The Hannah Cry - Birthing Purpose in the Barren Places
Diane Ferreira

Vale & Vine Press

Cover Design by Diane FerreiraInterior Design by Diane FerreiraEdited by Vale & Vine Press

ISBN: 979-8-9993872-2-6

Library of Congress Control Number: 2025942530

Published by Vale & Vine Press - Vale & Vine Books, Cromwell, Connecticut

Printed in the United States of America.

Dedication

To every woman who's ever carried something heavy, prayed through something impossible, and delivered something only God could bring forth.

And to my family: my husband Dave, my children, and the world's most entitled bulldog. You've loved me, supported me, and made room for this call. This book carries your fingerprints too.

All glory to the God who never wastes a single contraction.

Contents

Chapter 1
THE HANNAH CRY: WHEN PURPOSE GETS HEAVY

Let's not play cute. Purpose sounds beautiful on paper until you're actually carrying it. That's when it gets heavy.

Nobody talks about the part where you say yes to God, you obey, you trust, and... nothing happens. You're just standing there, looking around, wondering if Heaven lost your file. Because surely, if God had the right paperwork, this thing would have moved by now. But instead, you're pacing, praying, and feeling like you got left on read.

Welcome to what I call the Hannah Cry.

WHAT MAKES THIS CRY DIFFERENT

This isn't the little church prayer where you bow your head, recite your well-rehearsed request, and go on with your day like you're crossing items off a grocery list. No. This is the cry that shows up when your soul gets tired of pretending you're fine.

Hannah didn't show up at the temple with a cute request. The Bible says she prayed with "deep anguish" and "weeping bitterly." That's not casual. That's not polished. That's raw.

This is the prayer that leaks out when your emotions have worn you out and your strength clocked out five exits ago.

This is when you stop trying to impress God and start telling the truth.

YOU CAN BE ANOINTED AND ANGUISHED

Some of you have been told that real faith doesn't feel like this. That if you were really trusting God, you wouldn't be this upset. That's not biblical. That's just bad teaching.

Hannah was favored, chosen, anointed. And she was a mess.

Faith is not proven by your ability to suppress emotion. Faith shows up in the middle of your tears, when you keep bringing the same prayer back to God even though it hurts to say it again.

Faith is what keeps you walking into the sanctuary when your womb is still empty.

PURPOSE ALWAYS CARRIES A COST

Hannah wanted a child. God wanted a prophet. They were both after the same outcome, but for very different reasons.

See, that's the thing about divine assignments. You think you're praying for your desire, but Heaven is working on a whole different level.

You see lack. God sees legacy.

You see what you want now. God sees what He wants for generations after you're gone.

Hannah didn't know she was carrying Samuel. She just knew she was tired of crying.

THE SHIFT FROM "GIVE ME" TO "USE ME"

At some point, the prayer changed. And that's what moved Heaven.

Hannah stopped praying "Lord, give me" and started praying "Lord, if You give it, You can have it." That right there is where most people never get.

We want God to bless us. We just don't always want to let go of what the blessing is supposed to look like.

Hannah handed it over before she ever saw it.

That's what unlocked her womb.

IF YOU WANT TO CARRY PURPOSE, LEARN TO RELEASE CONTROL

Control will keep you stuck longer than the enemy ever could. God isn't fighting you for the promise. He's waiting for you to stop fighting Him for the steering wheel.

You can't control the timeline. You can't manipulate the outcome. You can't manufacture favor.

What you *can* do is surrender.

Real surrender sounds like this: "Lord, I'll carry it. I'll protect it. I'll deliver it. But You own it."

THIS IS YOUR HANNAH MOMENT

You're not reading this because you're empty. You're reading this because you're pregnant. You're carrying something you can't explain to most people. And let's be honest, you're tired.

You've done the praying. The fasting. The journaling. The obedience. And still, no delivery.

I know you want the promise. I know you're exhausted from the waiting. But what you're carrying is bigger than you.

This isn't about your comfort. It's about His purpose.

So now comes the moment where you make the shift. The prayer shifts. The posture shifts. The control shifts.

This is your Hannah Cry.

Not the cry of desperation. The cry of release.

PRAYER

Lord, I release my grip. I release my need to control how and when You move. I surrender this assignment back to You. If You've planted it, You'll birth it. Give me the strength to carry what You've entrusted to me. Teach me how to protect it while I wait. And when it's time to deliver, let it bring You glory far beyond anything I could have imagined. In Jesus' name, Amen.

REFLECTION QUESTIONS

1. What assignment has God planted inside of you that still feels

delayed?

2. Where have you tried to control outcomes instead of surrendering them?

3. What would full release look like for you right now?

4. Write out your own Hannah Cry prayer in your words. Be real. Be honest.

Chapter 2
THE SEED: GOD DROPS IT BEFORE YOU'RE READY

Let me help you out right from the start: God doesn't wait until you feel ready before He assigns something to you. If He did, none of us would be carrying anything.

Read your Bible. Nobody was ready.

Hannah wasn't ready for her assignment. She was empty. She was frustrated. She was overwhelmed. But God was already positioning her to carry something that didn't exist yet.

God drops the seed when He knows it's time. Not when you feel prepared.

STOP WAITING TO FEEL READY

If you're sitting around thinking, "I just need to get myself together before I step into this calling," you might want to go ahead and cancel that. Because God's not asking you for your perfection. He's asking for your participation.

Read that again.

He's not waiting for you to have it all figured out. He's not expecting you to be fully emotionally healed, debt-free, fully networked, with a pristine website, perfect confidence, and a 5-year plan.

Nope. That's your plan. Not His.

God drops the seed into women who are simply available. That's the qualifier.

THE SEED GETS DROPPED IN PRIVATE

Hannah's assignment didn't start on the delivery table. It started in the sanctuary, when nobody was paying attention.

Some of you are under the impression that God's next move for your life will be announced with fanfare, fireworks, and an Instagram Live.

Wrong.

Assignments get conceived when you're weeping in prayer while everyone else thinks you're losing your mind.

They don't see the seed drop. They only see the fruit later.

That's why you can't let the lack of applause make you question whether something's happening. Conception doesn't come with applause. It comes with obedience.

YOU DON'T GET TO PICK THE TIMELINE

Let's talk about your little planner for a second. You've got your timeline drawn up. You've got the dates circled. You've got the vision board. You've got the "I'll do this by 40" plan.

That's cute. But if you belong to God, your timeline is on the altar.

Hannah didn't know when. She just knew Who.

You're not being punished because it hasn't happened yet. You're being prepared to carry something heavier than you originally imagined.

That's why He had to plant the seed before you were ready. If He had waited for you to feel qualified, the assignment would have expired.

EVERY ASSIGNMENT HAS A SEED FORM

Let me be clear here. When God gives you an assignment, He rarely hands it to you fully developed. He gives you the seed, not the full tree.

You want the ministry. He gives you a burden for women.

You want the business. He gives you an idea that wakes you up at 2 AM.

You want the marriage. He gives you healing work to do first.

You want the platform. He gives you silence so you'll build your prayer life first.

Seeds don't look like what you're praying for. Seeds are messy, small, and unimpressive. But they carry everything inside of them for the full harvest...if you steward them right.

YOU WON'T ALWAYS UNDERSTAND IT IN THE BEGINNING

You're not supposed to understand the full blueprint at seed level. That's why it's called faith.

You don't get the final picture before you say yes. You get just enough light for the next step. And trust me, that's mercy. If God showed you everything attached to the assignment, you'd run like Jonah before you ever got started.

God gives you seed form because He's not just growing the assignment. He's growing you while you carry it.

DON'T ABANDON IT BECAUSE IT'S SMALL

This is where a lot of people lose it. They dismiss what God planted because it doesn't look like much right now. They abandon the assignment at seed level because it hasn't made them famous yet.

You're not called to chase applause. You're called to steward what God planted.

You nurture the seed in prayer. You protect it with obedience. You guard it with discernment.

And when it's time, the fruit will come.

THIS IS YOUR SEED SEASON

If you're reading this and thinking, "I don't see much happening," good. That's the point.

The seed is planted beneath the surface long before you see the breakthrough above it.

Don't confuse silence with inactivity. Just because people can't see it doesn't mean God isn't working.

You're pregnant. You just haven't shown yet.

PRAYER

Lord, I receive what You've planted. I release my obsession with the timeline. I surrender my need to understand the whole plan. Teach me to steward the seed while it's small. Grow me while You grow the assignment. Let me be faithful in private before You reveal it in public. In Jesus' name, Amen.

REFLECTION QUESTIONS

1. What seed do you believe God has planted in you that doesn't look like much yet?

2. Where have you struggled with impatience or frustration because you don't see results?

3. How can you start stewarding your seed assignment today, even before it fully develops?

Chapter 3
THE WEIGHT OF THE ASSIGNMENT: YOU ASKED FOR THIS, REMEMBER?

Let's have an honest conversation before you start side-eyeing God.

You prayed for this.

You sat in your prayer closet, journal open, worship music playing, telling God, "Use me." You said, "I surrender." You said, "I'm ready." You wrote out the vision. You made the Pinterest board. You fasted. You posted the cute little faith captions.

And now that God actually handed you the assignment, you're looking at Him like, "Wait. You were serious?"

Yes. He was serious.

YOU WANTED THE OIL BUT FORGOT ABOUT THE PRESS

Everybody wants the platform. Everybody wants to fulfill their purpose. Everybody wants to be anointed.

What most people don't want is the weight that comes with it.

You don't get oil without pressure. You don't get anointing without crushing. You don't get spiritual authority without some nights on your face, wondering if you even heard God right.

You asked for the assignment. Now you're being shaped to carry it.

THE BIGGER THE ASSIGNMENT, THE HEAVIER THE CARRY

You think the weight means God's mad at you. You think you did something wrong.

Let me help you.

The weight is confirmation, not condemnation.

If the assignment was light, you'd handle it in your flesh. God never lets you carry purpose that way. That's why He lets you feel the stretch.

The stretching builds your capacity. The pressure reveals your real motives. The discomfort drives you into deeper surrender.

You're not being crushed because you're failing. You're being crushed because He's preparing you.

NOBODY TALKS ABOUT THIS PART

See, this is the part they don't put on the conference flyer. This is the part nobody brags about on Instagram.

Nobody tells you that saying yes to God might cost you some relationships. Nobody tells you that people you thought were safe will get weird when you step into your assignment. Nobody tells you that walking in purpose feels like losing before it looks like winning.

You thought your yes was going to bring instant applause. But real assignments often start in silence.

THE SILENCE DOESN'T MEAN YOU'RE STUCK

God isn't ignoring you. He's insulating you.

There are seasons where God will limit your access to people, platforms, and opportunities because you're not ready yet...or better yet, because *they're* not ready to handle what you're carrying.

Hannah had to walk through the years of barrenness so that when the promise came, she would know exactly where it came from. No one else would be able to take credit for Samuel but God.

IT'S HEAVY BECAUSE IT'S HOLY

You want purpose? You want legacy? You want to birth what God put in you? Good.

But understand this: anything that carries eternal weight will feel heavy in your hands. That's why you need Him to carry it with you.

Your shoulders weren't built for this by themselves. His grace strengthens what your strength can't handle.

THE WEIGHT ISN'T GOING ANYWHERE, BUT NEITHER IS HIS GRACE

Let's go ahead and tell the truth: the assignment is never going to feel light. You're just going to grow stronger.

The same way a woman adjusts to carrying a pregnancy, your spirit adjusts to carrying purpose. What felt unbearable at first eventually becomes normal, not because the load changed, but because you did.

You won't break under this. You're being built under this.

PRAYER

Lord, I feel the weight of what You've entrusted to me. Help me not to resent the responsibility. Strengthen me to carry it with grace and wisdom. Strip away every selfish motive so that what I birth will glorify You alone. Teach me how to endure the pressure without losing my peace. I trust that if You planted this assignment in me, You will sustain me through it. In Jesus' name, Amen.

REFLECTION QUESTIONS

1. Where have you felt overwhelmed by the weight of your assignment?

2. What emotions or fears have surfaced as you've stepped deeper into your calling?

3. How can you lean into God's grace when you feel stretched beyond your strength?

Chapter 4
WHEN GOD GETS QUIET: YOU'RE NOT GHOSTED, YOU'RE GUARDED

One of the hardest parts of carrying purpose is when God stops talking.

You're praying. You're fasting. You're journaling. You're doing everything you know to do. But Heaven goes silent. The same God who gave you the assignment suddenly feels out of office.

That silence will make you question everything.

Did I miss something? Did I do something wrong? Am I being punished?

But it's not punishment you are feeling, it is development.

SILENCE IS PART OF THE PROCESS

When God goes quiet, He is not absent. He is present in a different way. He shifts from speaking to observing. He watches how you handle the instructions you already received.

Silence is not rejection. Silence is assessment. The teacher does not give answers during the test. The teacher watches.

You are in a testing season. Your faith, obedience, patience, and trust are being evaluated.

THE ENEMY LOVES TO FILL THE QUIET

Satan will not miss his opportunity. When God goes silent, the enemy starts whispering.

He feeds you lies that sound like logic.

"If God really called you, this wouldn't feel like this.""You probably missed your chance.""Maybe you misunderstood what He said.""Look at how easy it's happening for her."

Oh, does that ever sound familiar!

The enemy's goal is not to steal your promise. He cannot do that. His goal is to make you abandon it yourself out of fear, frustration, or fatigue.

Your job in the silence is to hold your position. When there are no new orders, you keep obeying the last one you received.

THE SILENCE EXPOSES WHAT YOU BELIEVE

It is easy to trust God when He is speaking. It is different when you have to trust who He is while you hear nothing.

The silence reveals if you trust His voice or His character.

Do you believe He is faithful, even when you do not feel Him? Do you trust that He is still working when you see no movement? Can you stay planted without constant reassurance?

The silence exposes your foundation.

GOD USES SILENCE TO PROTECT YOU

Sometimes God goes quiet because He knows you are not ready to handle the full picture.

You pray for clarity. As I said before, God gives you just enough light for the next step. If He showed you everything right now, you would either run from it or try to control it. He withholds information to protect you from sabotaging your own assignment.

The silence is not punishment. It is mercy.

YOUR SILENCE IS STILL BEING SEEN

Hannah prayed for years before anything changed. The text does not tell us how many times she walked into that sanctuary empty-handed. We only know the day God moved.

Her waiting years were not wasted years. Every silent season prepared her for the moment of fulfillment.

God was not ignoring her. He was guarding the promise.

That is where you are.

You think you are being overlooked. You are being hidden.

Hidden seasons are holy seasons. God hides what He is growing so it will not be tampered with before its time.

DON'T MOVE BECAUSE YOU'RE UNCOMFORT-ABLE

This is the danger in silence. You will be tempted to force movement. You will want to create your own opportunities. You will want to birth your own Ishmael. You will want to kick down doors that God has not opened yet.

Forced doors require forced maintenance. What you manufacture, you have to sustain. What God opens, He upholds.

Sit still. Obey the last instruction. Let Him be God.

YOU ARE STILL COVERED

You do not have to feel Him to be held by Him.

The silence is not a signal to panic. It is an invitation to trust. God knows exactly where you are. He has not changed His mind about what He assigned to you. He is preparing the environment around you and maturing what is inside you.

Hold your position. Stay planted. The silence will not last forever.

PRAYER

Lord, I admit the silence makes me uncomfortable. I want answers. I want movement. I want confirmation. But I choose to trust You even when I do not hear You. Strengthen me to remain obedient while I wait. Guard my mind from lies that make me question what You have spoken. Hide me while You prepare the promise. I will not abandon what You have assigned to me. In Jesus' name, Amen.

REFLECTION QUESTIONS

1. Where have you been struggling with God's silence?

2. What lies have tried to fill the space where God feels quiet?

3. How can you stay anchored in God's character while you wait?

Chapter 5
THE COMPARISON TRAP: STAY OUT OF EVERYBODY ELSE'S LANE

Nothing will drain your confidence like watching somebody else win while you are still waiting for your turn.

It starts small. You congratulate her. You mean it. You really do.

But somewhere in the back of your mind, you are having a little side conversation with God.

"So, Lord. I see You handing out assignments today. That's cute. You remember I'm still here, right? Just checking."

COMPARISON WILL CHOKE YOUR ASSIGNMENT

You are not delayed because someone else is succeeding. Their blessing has nothing to do with your timeline. God is not running out of miracles. He is not managing a limited inventory of open doors.

The fastest way to miss what God is doing in your life is to get so busy watching someone else that you forget to steward what He already gave you.

GOD NEVER CALLED YOU TO RUN HER RACE

You know why some women are exhausted? They are carrying assignments God never gave them. They keep trying to copy what looks successful on somebody else's platform.

Stop mimicking her branding.Stop studying her style. Stop following her formula like it holds the secret code.

You are not called to build a knockoff version of someone else's calling. You were assigned a lane that fits your oil, your voice, your audience, and your capacity. What works for her will collapse under you. You do not have the grace to carry someone else's assignment.

HER FRUIT IS NOT YOUR COMPETITION

You don't know the price she paid. You don't know the private fights she walked through to get what you are watching on your timeline.

You don't know the prayers she had to pray to survive the weight you envy.

Be careful envying a harvest you were never called to plant.

When you fix your eyes on what she's carrying, you will start mishandling what God planted in you.

Your focus determines your fruit.Your comparison delays your delivery.

COMPARISON IS A DISTRACTION STRATEGY

The enemy knows he cannot steal your assignment. His next best option is to keep you distracted long enough that you never deliver it.

He will bait you with the illusion that you are behind. He will make you question whether God forgot you. He will convince you that you have to catch up to her pace.

God's not measuring your progress against anyone else's timeline. He is measuring your obedience against what He assigned to you.

Your job is not to keep up. Your job is to stay faithful.

MIND YOUR OWN ASSIGNMENT

You don't need her audience. You don't need her connections. You don't need her opportunities. You need to master your own assignment.

When God is ready to elevate you, He will. When the door is ready, it will open. Until then, your job is to water your own seed.

Stay in your lane. Mind your own assignment. Protect your own oil.

SUCCESS IS NOT A LIMITED RESOURCE

Some of you act like God is handing out purpose on a clearance rack. Like if she grabs hers first, you're stuck with whatever scraps are left.

God doesn't operate in scarcity.

He is not limited by followers, algorithms, publishing deals, or speaking platforms. He creates new spaces that do not exist yet.

You are not in competition with anybody, and your purpose is not on a countdown clock.

THE CELEBRATION TEST

How you handle someone else's harvest reveals a lot about your heart. If you can't clap for her in her winning season, you are not ready for your own. You will not sabotage what God has for you by celebrating what He gave to her.

Jealousy delays. Honor accelerates.

Learn to clap with genuine joy.God is not overlooking you. He is observing you.

PRAYER

Lord, help me keep my eyes on what You have assigned to me. I release every comparison, every silent competition, and every insecure thought that tries to steal my peace. Strengthen me to steward what You have planted without distraction. Teach me how to celebrate others while trusting You for my own harvest. I will stay in my lane. I will guard my focus. I will trust Your timing. In Jesus' name, Amen.

REFLECTION QUESTIONS

1. Where have you been tempted to compare your assignment to someone else's?

2. How has comparison affected your ability to focus on your assignment?

3. What specific steps can you take to protect your peace and stay in your lane?

Chapter 6
WOMB WARFARE: THE ATTACK ON WHAT YOU HAVEN'T DELIVERED YET

You think you're being attacked because of where you are right now. You're not. You're being attacked because of what you're carrying. Hell isn't reacting to your current status. Hell is reacting to your future.

You're still in the carrying phase. You don't have anything to show yet. There's no fruit on display. But the enemy isn't stupid. He can see what you can't. He recognizes the assignment developing inside you even while you're still wondering if you made it up.

You don't feel dangerous. You feel tired. But from hell's perspective, you are lethal.

WAR STARTS EARLY

The enemy doesn't wait for the delivery to launch his attack. He starts while the promise is still in seed form. You know why? Because it's easier to get you to abandon something you haven't seen yet.

Think about Herod in Matthew 2. The Messiah had just been born. No miracles performed yet. No sermons preached. No disciples gathered.

But Herod was already trying to kill Him. Why? Because the threat wasn't about what Jesus had done. The threat was who He was going to become.

It's the same with you. The enemy isn't reacting to your platform, your following, or your fruit. He's reacting to your potential.

WHEN THE ATTACK DOESN'T FEEL LIKE AN ATTACK

Womb warfare is sneaky because it doesn't always feel like warfare. You expect the enemy to show up obvious, with his horns and pitchfork. You expect crisis. You expect big, loud drama.

Instead, you get slow, steady erosion.

One day you're sure. The next you're not. One minute you're fired up. The next you're discouraged. One morning you're motivated. By afternoon, you're overwhelmed.

You may think that's mood swings. It's not... that's strategy. His goal is not to destroy you with one blow. His goal is to wear you out little by little until you convince yourself it's easier to quit than to fight.

YOUR MIND IS THE BATTLEFIELD

You're not physically under attack. Your mind is.

The questions start creeping in. "Did God really call me to this?" "Am I qualified for this?" "What if I'm just wasting my time?" "Maybe this was just a good idea, not a God idea."

The longer you sit in those questions, the heavier they get. You start trying to logic your way out of something you were never supposed to analyze in the first place.

You can't strategize your way through spiritual warfare. You have to war through it.

DISTRACTION IS DISGUISED AS OPPORTUNITY

When discouragement doesn't work, distraction steps in. The enemy doesn't need you to do something evil. He just needs you to get busy with things that don't serve your assignment.

The danger isn't always sin. Sometimes it's good things. Things that look productive. Things that look responsible. Things people will applaud you for.

It's not evil that is distracting you. You're distracted by options. And every time you divert your attention, you slow down the development of what God planted.

Think about Nehemiah (Nehemiah 6:3). His enemies kept trying to pull him off the wall with fake meetings and conversations. His response was simple. "I am doing a great work, so I cannot come down." That's your assignment. Stay on the wall.

THE LONGER YOU CARRY, THE HARDER HE PUSHES

Time is one of the enemy's favorite weapons. He knows most people don't have the patience to carry something long-term without progress. So he plays the waiting game. He lets you get tired.

When the delay stretches, he whispers louder. "Maybe this wasn't God.""Maybe it's too late.""Maybe you missed your moment."

Delay is not denial. Delay is development. But the enemy hopes you'll confuse the two.

THIS ISN'T PERSONAL. IT'S STRATEGIC.

You need to settle this right now. You're not under attack because you're weak. You're under attack because what you're carrying is valuable.

Hell doesn't waste resources on people who aren't a threat.

When you feel the pressure increasing, that's confirmation that you are on schedule. If there was no fight, you'd have to question whether you're even carrying anything.

YOU ARE NOT POWERLESS

You don't have to sit there and take the attack like a victim. God gave you authority over what He assigned to you. You don't fight this battle by complaining. You fight by protecting the space where the promise is developing.

You guard your mind. You guard your circle. You guard your routine. You guard your input.

You stay out of conversations that feed your fear. You shut down voices that question your assignment. You limit access to people who drain your faith. This is your responsibility.

Proverbs 4:23 says it simply.

"Guard your heart diligently, for from it flow the springs of life."

In this season, your job is to guard what God gave you like your life depends on it. Because it does.

HELL DOESN'T WIN UNLESS YOU WALK AWAY

The enemy cannot take what God planted. He has no authority to steal your assignment. All he can do is try to convince you to abandon it.

You're still carrying. You're still breathing. You're still here. That's proof he hasn't won.

Stand your ground. Protect your womb. Refuse to walk away from what God called you to deliver. You are further along than you think.

PRAYER

Lord, I see the attack for what it is. The enemy is after what You have planted, but I will not abandon my assignment. Strengthen my mind to resist every lie and distraction. Help me guard what You've entrusted to me. Expose every strategy that tries to wear me down. I declare that I will carry this to full term. In Jesus' name, Amen.

REFLECTION QUESTIONS

1. What specific distractions have pulled your attention away from your assignment?

2. Where have you seen the enemy try to wear you down mentally?

3. What boundaries do you need to set to protect the space where your assignment is developing?

Chapter 7
PEOPLE YOU CAN'T TAKE INTO LABOR

Everybody loves the idea of you birthing purpose.

Until it's time for you to actually push.

That's when the room starts getting really small.

When you start carrying something from God, you learn quickly that not everyone around you can handle what you're carrying. Some people were fine when you were barren. They clapped while you were frustrated. They loved praying for you when nothing was moving. But now that the promise is developing, their energy has shifted.

The truth is that labor requires privacy. Some people cannot handle seeing you deliver.

LABOR IS INTIMATE

When a woman goes into labor, not everyone is invited into the delivery room.

Why? Because labor is vulnerable. Labor exposes you. Labor is messy. Labor strips away the filters and the pretense. It's not pretty...it's beautiful, but not pretty.

You are wide open, exhausted, and fully dependent on God to get the assignment out of you. That environment is not for spectators. That space is for people who are equipped to support you, not distract you.

Jesus modeled this with Jairus' daughter in Mark 5:37-40. Before He raised her, He cleared the room. He allowed only Peter, James, and John to stay. He put the mockers out. Some people cannot witness resurrection. They don't have the capacity to believe for what's about to happen.

NOT EVERY FRIEND IS A MIDWIFE

Ooh, I love this one... so stay with me!

Just because someone loves you doesn't mean they're assigned to help you deliver.

You have friends who are wonderful for brunch, great for small talk, helpful for errands, and even spiritually supportive when life is light.

But when you step into labor, you need more than good company. You need people with spiritual endurance.

You need women who know how to war in prayer, who will not get nervous when the contractions intensify. You need people who understand that when you say, "I can't do this," they speak life instead of agreeing with your exhaustion.

SOME PEOPLE ARE SILENTLY INTIMIDATED

Let's go ahead and deal with the part nobody says out loud.

Some people were fine with you when you were stuck. They were comfortable when you were still praying for the thing you're now carrying. They were secure when you were empty because your emptiness made their comfort feel spiritual.

Now that God is growing something in you, they are privately uncomfortable. They don't say it. But their passive comments shift. Their support becomes inconsistent. Their encouragement gets dry.

They are not angry. They are intimidated.

Luke 1:39-45 gives us the opposite picture. When Mary visited Elizabeth, the baby in Elizabeth's womb leapt. That is what healthy alignment feels like. The right people respond to what you are carrying with joy, not jealousy.

WHO YOU LET IN AFFECTS THE DELIVERY

Your birthing room isn't just about comfort. It's about atmosphere.

The wrong people bring doubt. The wrong people carry anxiety. The wrong people question timing. The wrong people insert opinions that feed your insecurity.

One nervous voice in the wrong moment can cost you your peace.

You are not being rude when you guard access. You are being responsible.

THIS IS NOT THE SEASON FOR EXPLAINING

You don't owe everybody an explanation for why they don't have access right now. You are not obligated to walk people through your decision to protect what God is doing in you.

Labor is not the time to debate who belongs. Labor is the time to focus on the delivery.

The people assigned to help you push will already know their role. They won't need convincing. They won't make it about themselves. They will bring towels and water, not questions and opinions.

SOME PEOPLE WERE NEVER SUPPOSED TO STAY

Let's tell the truth, even if it stings a little.

Some people were only assigned to your waiting season.

They were part of your story while you were still becoming. They were assigned to the version of you who was praying for the assignment, not the version of you who is about to deliver it.

And that's fine. Not everyone is meant to go the whole way. The problem comes when you keep holding space for people God is trying to release. You feel obligated. They feel entitled. And your assignment pays the price.

PROTECT THE ROOM

You cannot afford emotional negotiations when your assignment is at stake.

This is the moment where you draw clear boundaries. Not out of offense. Not out of pettiness. Out of obedience.

Your birthing room is holy ground. The people allowed to stay in that room should carry the weight with you in prayer, stand with you in faith, and speak life when your strength gets low.

They need to believe when you can't. They need to remind you when you forget. They need to carry towels, not judgment.

IF THEY CAN'T HANDLE THE LABOR, THEY DON'T GET TO HOLD THE BABY

Read that again. Slowly.

If they do not have the faith to labor with you, they do not get the access to enjoy the fruit when it arrives.

You are not being harsh. You are stewarding what God assigned.

This assignment is too heavy, too costly, and too holy to be jeopardized by people who only want front row seats but no labor pains.

PRAYER

Lord, give me wisdom to discern who belongs in my birthing room. Remove every voice that feeds my fear or doubts my assignment. Surround me with people who carry the weight with me in prayer. Strengthen my discernment to protect what You are doing in this season. I will not negotiate access where You have called for separation. Help me release who no longer belongs so I can fully deliver what You've planted.In Jesus' name, Amen.

REFLECTION QUESTIONS

1. Who in your circle supports your assignment and strengthens your faith?

2. Who in your circle drains your peace or plants doubt?

3. What boundaries do you need to put in place to protect your delivery season?

Chapter 8

THE FEAR FACTOR: WHEN WHAT YOU CARRY SCARES YOU

Nobody likes to admit this part, but here we are.

Sometimes it's not the waiting that scares you. It's the weight.

It's not the uncertainty about whether God can do it. It's the realization that He might actually do it. And when He does, you are the one who will have to carry it, protect it, and lead it.

This is the part that church people don't always talk about. You prayed for this. You asked for this. But now that you're carrying it, you're low-key terrified.

YOU WEREN'T SCARED WHEN IT WAS JUST AN IDEA

It's easy to feel bold when it's all theory. Vision boards feel safe. Planning feels productive. Talking about purpose feels exciting.

But when God starts actually moving, the real pressure shows up. That's when you realize this is bigger than a cute Instagram caption. This requires obedience at a level you didn't anticipate.

God gives you the seed. That part is exciting. But as it grows, so does your responsibility.

The bigger it gets, the more exposed you feel. The more exposed you feel, the more your fear starts talking.

FEAR DOESN'T ALWAYS SOUND LIKE FEAR

Fear doesn't always come through the front door screaming. It shows up dressed like wisdom.

"I need more time." "I'm just waiting on more confirmation." "I don't want to move ahead of God." "I'm being careful."

There's nothing wrong with wisdom, but don't confuse wisdom with hesitation wrapped in spiritual language. Some of what you call caution is actually fear hiding behind Christian vocabulary.

FEAR WILL MAKE YOU FORGET WHO CALLED YOU

You start to question your own authority. "Am I really called to this?" "Who do I think I am to lead this?" "What if I fail and everyone sees it?"

This isn't humility. This is intimidation. Fear knows that if you keep questioning your ability, you will eventually question God's assignment.

Moses did the same thing at the burning bush. God called him directly. Gave him the plan. Showed him signs. And Moses still responded with ***"Who am I that I should go?"*** (Exodus 3:11).

Moses wasn't confused. He was scared.

THE BIGGER THE ASSIGNMENT, THE LOUDER THE FEAR

There's a reason the enemy turns up the volume when you get close to delivery. He knows if you step into this fully, the ripple effect will outlive you.

He's not just trying to intimidate you for today. He's trying to stop what you're carrying from ever reaching the people it's assigned to serve.

Your assignment carries generational weight. That's why it feels heavy. That's why you feel the resistance. It's not because you're doing something wrong. It's because you're right on schedule.

FEAR LOVES COMPANY

Be careful who you process your fear with. Not everybody can handle hearing your insecurities without feeding them.

Some people will start listing every reason why you should pull back. They'll remind you of your failures. They'll bring up your weaknesses. They'll question your qualifications.

They think they're being helpful. But really, they're partnering with your fear.

This is why God had to shut Zechariah up when he doubted the promise of John's birth (Luke 1:18-20). God knew his mouth could interfere with the delivery if He let him keep speaking. Sometimes God has to silence people who don't have the faith to match your assignment.

GOD IS NOT OBLIGATED TO MAKE YOU FEEL READY

We keep waiting for peace to show up before we move forward. But God does not owe you the feeling of readiness before He expects your obedience.

The peace you want usually comes after you step, not before.

You're asking for the nerves to disappear. God is asking for your yes in spite of them. That's how faith works.

If you only obey when you feel fully confident, you'll never move. Fear doesn't mean you're not called. It means you're human.

FEAR SHRINKS WHEN YOU MOVE

Here's the part fear doesn't want you to figure out. The longer you sit still, the stronger fear gets. The moment you start moving, fear loses power.

The more you obey, the smaller fear becomes. The more you delay, the louder it screams.

You don't conquer fear by praying it away. You conquer it by walking anyway.

Ask Joshua. After Moses died, God told him repeatedly, ***"Be strong. Be courageous."*** (Joshua 1). God wasn't offering him reassurance. God was commanding him to move even while he felt intimidated.

THE FEAR ISN'T GOING TO KILL YOU

Let's get real practical.

You are not going to die from feeling scared. You are not going to crumble because your hands are shaking. You will not fail because your stomach is tight.

You've survived worse than this.

The only thing fear can destroy is the assignment you refuse to carry because you listened to it.

GOD TRUSTED YOU WITH THIS FOR A REASON

He knew your weaknesses when He chose you. He saw your insecurities before He assigned you. He factored in your doubts before He planted the seed.

He still gave it to you.

You're not carrying this by accident. You're carrying it because He trusted you to steward it. Your job is not to eliminate fear. Your job is to refuse to let fear lead.

PRAYER

Lord, I acknowledge my fear but I refuse to bow to it. I surrender every excuse, hesitation, and insecurity. I trust that You chose me on purpose. I will not delay obedience waiting to feel ready. Strengthen my faith as I move forward. I will carry what You've given me with courage. In Jesus' name, Amen.

REFLECTION QUESTIONS

1. Where has fear caused you to hesitate in your assignment?

2. What excuses have you been using that sound like wisdom but are really fear?

3. What is one step you can take this week to move forward despite fear?

Chapter 9

FALSE LABOR: WHEN YOU TRY TO PUSH BEFORE GOD SAYS IT'S TIME

You've been carrying your assignment for a while now. You've prayed. You've fasted. You've cried. You've journaled. You've been obedient. And somewhere in all of that, the thought starts creeping in:

"Maybe I should just go ahead and make something happen."

That right there is where most people start confusing movement with progress. You're not disobedient. You're just tired of waiting. You start feeling like you've carried long enough. So, you start looking for a shortcut. Something that feels close enough to purpose that you can call it obedience but still satisfies your impatience.

Welcome to false labor.

FALSE LABOR FEELS REAL UNTIL IT ISN'T

In the natural, false labor looks and feels a lot like the real thing. The contractions hit. The pressure builds. The symptoms line up. But nothing is actually happening. No delivery is taking place.

Spiritually, it's no different.

You feel the tension building. You feel like you're ready to release what you've been carrying. But when you try to force it, nothing comes forth. You end up drained, discouraged, and sometimes embarrassed because you stepped before God gave clearance.

It looked like a good move. It sounded like a God move. But it wasn't His timing.

GOD'S TIMING ISN'T BASED ON YOUR COM-FORT LEVEL

One of the most dangerous mindsets is assuming that just because you're uncomfortable, it must mean God is ready to deliver you from the waiting. Discomfort doesn't equal clearance.

God doesn't operate off of your frustration level. He operates off of fullness of time.

Galatians 4:4 makes that crystal clear.

"But when the fullness of time had come, God sent His Son."

Jesus didn't show up when people got tired of waiting for a Messiah. He showed up when Heaven declared it was time.

The same applies to your assignment. You can't rush fullness.

SARAH AND HAGAR - A CLASSIC FALSE LABOR STORY

If you need a perfect biblical picture of false labor, you don't have to look any further than Sarah and Hagar.

God had promised Abraham and Sarah a son. The assignment was real. The promise was guaranteed. But the wait got long. Sarah grew tired of feeling like nothing was happening, so she came up with her own plan.

She offered her servant Hagar to Abraham as a workaround. Hagar got pregnant quickly. It looked like progress. It looked like God's promise had been delivered.

But it wasn't the promise, it was a product of impatience. And it caused nothing but conflict, division, and unnecessary pain.

That's what false labor produces. It births situations that require damage control later.

FALSE LABOR IS USUALLY ROOTED IN PRIDE

Most of the time, false labor isn't about the assignment itself. It's about your ego.

You want the discomfort to end. You want the applause that comes with the delivery. You want the relief of finally having something to show for all this carrying.

But underneath all of that is a quiet pride that says, "I'm ready. God must be dragging His feet."

That mindset will have you launching businesses, ministries, books, and platforms that God never authorized. And when they flop or drain you, you'll blame the enemy, but you were the one who pushed before clearance was given.

THE ENEMY LOVES TO ENCOURAGE FALSE LABOR

You might assume that the enemy always tries to delay you. Not necessarily. Sometimes, he's more than happy to encourage you to run ahead of God.

He'll send people to cheer you on prematurely. He'll open doors that weren't assigned to you. He'll manufacture opportunities that feel like favor but are actually distractions.

Premature promotion is still a trap.

Satan isn't concerned with whether you're moving. He's concerned with whether you're aligned. You can be active and completely out of order.

YOU CAN'T DELIVER WHAT HASN'T FINISHED DEVELOPING

There is a reason babies stay in the womb for nine months. There's reason certain assignments sit in the secret place longer than you want them to.

If you try to push something out too soon, it won't survive the pressure outside the womb. The weight, the warfare, the exposure... it would crush an undeveloped promise.

Premature delivery leads to unnecessary maintenance. You'll find yourself constantly resuscitating something that should have been carried longer before release.

Ecclesiastes 3:1 says it plainly.

"For everything there is a season, and a time for every activity under heaven."

WAITING ISN'T PUNISHMENT. IT'S PROTECTION.

The waiting is refining you. It's strengthening the assignment. It's aligning the right people, the right resources, the right opportunities. What feels like delay is actually preparation.

God isn't trying to frustrate you. He's preserving you. He's setting you up to sustain what you're about to release. Because once it's delivered, you'll have to steward it. You won't be able to put it back inside.

This is not punishment. This is mercy.

THE ROOM WILL OPEN WHEN HE SAYS SO

You won't have to force your way in when it's time. The doors will open on schedule. The release will come with peace, not panic. The delivery will flow, not fight you.

Isaiah 66:9 says:

"Shall I bring to the point of birth and not cause delivery? says Adonai."

When God gives clearance, there won't be confusion. You won't need manipulation. You won't have to hustle to make it happen. What's been developing in secret will come forth publicly under His covering.

PRAYER

Lord, I release my desire to control the timeline. I surrender my impatience and pride. I trust Your timing even when I don't understand it. Guard me from false opportunities that look like progress but lead to distraction. Strengthen me to carry this assignment to full term. I will not move ahead of Your schedule. In Jesus' name, Amen.

REFLECTION QUESTIONS

1. Where have you been tempted to move ahead of God's timing?

2. What doors have opened that feel like opportunity but may

not be assigned?

3. How can you guard your heart and your assignment while you wait for God's clearance?

Chapter 10
WARFARE IN THE WAITING ROOM

Waiting sounds peaceful when you say it out loud.

You make it sound spiritual. "I'm just waiting on the Lord." It sounds like you're sitting calmly, sipping tea, journaling deep thoughts, and humming worship songs while angels fan you with palm branches.

That's not waiting. That's your Instagram version.

Real waiting is warfare.

The waiting room is where most assignments get lost. Not because God changes His mind, but because we can't hold our position long enough for Him to release what He promised.

THE WAITING ROOM EXPOSES YOUR REAL FAITH

Everybody can believe when things are moving.

But when nothing is happening? That's where your faith shows up. The waiting room reveals whether you trust God or just trust momentum.

Waiting forces you to face the gap between what God said and what you see. That gap is where fear, doubt, and impatience try to move in and unpack.

This is why David said in Psalm 27:14

"Wait for Adonai. Be strong, let Your heart take courage, and wait for Adonai."

Courage isn't just for battlefields. You need courage to wait.

THE ENEMY USES THE CLOCK AGAINST YOU

The longer you sit in the waiting room, the louder the enemy talks.

He starts pulling out receipts."You should have been further along by now." "Other people are already doing what you're still dreaming about." "Maybe God changed His mind." "Maybe you missed your window."

He will weaponize your age, your calendar, your circumstances, and your emotions.

But here's the truth: God is not on your clock. His timing is not threatened by your birthday or your to-do list. Heaven operates on fullness, not frustration.

THE DANGER OF RESTLESS OBEDIENCE

Some people sit in the waiting room physically but not mentally. They're pacing in their minds. Strategizing ways to help God out. Planning scenarios just in case He needs a backup plan.

You might still be in place, but your mind is restless. And restless obedience eventually turns into rebellion if you're not careful.

The Israelites knew this well. Moses went up the mountain for 40 days. It didn't take long before the people got restless. They built a golden calf because waiting on God felt too uncertain. They didn't want to wait for His voice. They wanted something they could control. (Exodus 32)

That's how most detours start. You create substitutes while God is finishing the real thing.

THE WAITING ROOM TESTS YOUR STEWARD-SHIP

Waiting isn't passive. It's preparation.

You're not just sitting. You're being refined. You're being trained to steward what's coming. Because once it arrives, you won't have time to build your discipline. You'll have to operate in it.

If you mishandle your waiting season, you'll mishandle your delivery season.

Joseph spent years in waiting rooms. Betrayed by his brothers, sold into slavery, thrown into prison, forgotten by people who promised to help him. But every single delay was positioning him for authority. And when Pharaoh called, Joseph was ready.

He wasn't frustrated. He was prepared.

SILENCE IN THE WAITING ROOM IS NOT ABANDONMENT

There will be long stretches where God says nothing. No new word. No fresh confirmation. Just silence.

Silence doesn't mean He left the room.

Silence means He's letting the seed develop without your interference. Your job is not to hear constant updates. Your job is to hold your position in trust.

If God went silent, it's because He already spoke. Your next move is still obedience to the last thing He said.

YOU DON'T GRADUATE FROM THE WAITING ROOM. YOU GET RELEASED.

There's no exam to pass. You don't get extra credit for good behavior. You don't negotiate your way out.

The release date belongs to God.

When He opens the door, no one can close it. And when He hasn't opened it yet, no one can force it open.

Isaiah 40:31 says:

> *"But they who wait for Adonai will renew their strength."*

Waiting doesn't drain you. Fighting God's timing does. When you wait right, you get stronger.

THE LONGER THE WAIT, THE HEAVIER THE WEIGHT

You don't like hearing this, but you need to hear it.

If God is letting you sit in the waiting room longer than you expected, it's because the assignment on the other side carries more weight than you realize.

He's not being cruel. He's being kind. He's not stalling you. He's strengthening you.

When the door finally opens, you won't have to scramble to catch up. You'll be equipped to walk straight into what you've been carrying.

PRAYER

Lord, I surrender my timeline to You. Strengthen my heart while I wait. Silence every lie that tries to discourage me. I trust that You are preparing me for what You've promised. I will not create substitutes to satisfy my impatience. I will wait in faith, knowing You are always on time. In Jesus' name, Amen.

REFLECTION QUESTIONS

1. Where have you struggled with restlessness while waiting?

2. How has the enemy tried to use time against you?

3. What spiritual disciplines can you build while you wait to prepare for what's coming?

Chapter 11
LABOR PAINS: STRETCHING YOU BEFORE YOU PUSH

Everybody wants the promise. Until the pressure hits.

You pray for purpose. You pray for increase. You pray for God to use you. That part feels holy. That part feels safe. But what you're not always ready for is what comes next. The stretching.

Because God doesn't just drop assignments fully formed into your lap. He grows them in you. And that growth requires capacity you didn't think you needed.

Labor pains aren't punishment. They're preparation. They're stretching you to make room for what you're about to deliver.

PAIN DOESN'T MEAN SOMETHING'S WRONG

We've been conditioned to think that pain equals a problem. That if something hurts, something must be broken. But that's not true in labor.

The pain isn't a sign that something's going wrong. The pain is proof that something is progressing.

When contractions hit in natural labor, they don't mean the baby is in trouble. They mean the baby is moving into position.

You're not being punished. You're being positioned.

THE STRETCH IS UNCOMFORTABLE BECAUSE YOU HAVEN'T BEEN HERE BEFORE

You're stretching into capacity you've never carried before. That's why it feels foreign. You've never had to operate at this level yet. The weight feels strange. The pressure feels new.

This is where most people panic. They start mistaking growth for danger. They feel the pressure and immediately assume they need to change directions.

But the only thing you need to do right now is breathe and stay steady.

God is enlarging your capacity for what's coming. You prayed for influence. Now He's stretching your endurance. You prayed for the platform. Now He's stretching your character. You prayed for the assignment. Now He's stretching your faith.

THE STRETCH CAN FEEL LIKE ISOLATION

Let's deal with what nobody says.

The deeper you get into this stretching phase, the smaller your circle may feel. It's not that people abandoned you. It's that what you're carrying requires a level of focus and intimacy with God that can't be shared right now.

Jesus modeled this in Gethsemane. The closer He got to the cross, the fewer people stayed awake with Him. He brought three disciples with Him, but even they couldn't handle the weight of that moment. (Matthew 26:36-46)

Stretching seasons feel lonely because not everyone has the stamina to stay present while God is stretching you.

STRETCHING EXPOSES WHAT NEEDS TO BREAK

Sometimes God allows the pressure to expose what can't go with you into the next season.

During this phase, old habits, toxic mindsets, and hidden insecurities start bubbling up. That's not failure. That's exposure. God's letting the pressure bring to the surface what needs to break before you deliver.

You don't want to drag emotional baggage into delivery. You want to confront it now while you still have space to heal.

THERE'S A DIFFERENCE BETWEEN PAIN AND DAMAGE

As I said, not all pain is destructive. Some pain is developmental.

Think about going to the gym to work out for the first time. The next day, your body may ache in places you didn't even know could hurt like that.

Nothing is wrong...in fact it's just the opposite. You ache because your muscles are developing. They have to go through some pain to do so.

The enemy will try to convince you that the pressure means you're about to break. That's a lie. God knows exactly how much stretch you can handle. He's not reckless with your life.

Isaiah 42:3 says:

"A bruised reed He will not break, and a smoldering wick He will not snuff out."

God knows how to stretch you without snapping you.

He's building endurance you'll need once the promise arrives.

YOU CAN'T RUSH THE STRETCH

There is no shortcut through this phase. You can't pray it away. You can't fast your way around it. The only way out is through.

The stretching is happening for your benefit. You don't want to deliver something you aren't prepared to sustain. Growth without capacity creates collapse.

You asked God to trust you with something bigger. This is what bigger feels like.

THIS IS WHERE YOU LEARN TO BREATHE

In natural labor, breathing is everything. Not because it stops the pain, but because it keeps you steady in the middle of it.

Spiritually, it's the same.

When the pressure increases, you breathe. You return to prayer. You stay anchored in God's Word. You keep your rhythm steady. You don't let panic drive you. You keep breathing while God keeps stretching.

Psalm 61:2 says:

"From the end of the earth I call to You, when my heart is faint. Lead me to the rock that is higher than I."

When the pressure builds, you anchor yourself to the Rock.

PRAYER

Lord, the stretching is uncomfortable, but I trust You in it.Ex pand my capacity. Break what needs to be broken. Strengthen what needs to be strengthened.Keep me steady while You prepare me for what's coming.I will not run from the pressure. I will endure the stretch knowing that You are building me to carry what You've promised.In Jesus' name, Amen.

REFLECTION QUESTIONS

1. Where have you felt the pressure increasing as you prepare to deliver?

2. What mindsets or habits is God exposing in this stretching season?

3. How can you stay anchored while God increases your capacity?

Chapter 12
TRAVAIL: THE UGLY CRY THAT CHANGES EVERYTHING

Have you ever ugly cried? I have and it is called that for good reason; it is NOT pretty.

And this isn't the pretty kind of prayer.

This isn't the churchy prayer you say at women's conferences when the camera's rolling and your makeup is still intact.

Travail is not cute. It is not polished. It doesn't photograph well. Travail is the kind of cry that hits when you've run out of words, when you're not even sure what you're saying anymore, when your tears say what your mouth can't.

This is where real delivery begins.

TRAVAIL ISN'T A PRAYER FORMULA

Some people treat prayer like a script. They think the right combination of flowery words will move God faster.

Travail doesn't care about your word count. Travail is raw. Travail is spiritual labor. It's not about how loud you get. It's about how surrendered you are.

Hannah gave us this picture in 1 Samuel 1:10.

"While her soul was bitter, she prayed to Adonai and wept."

She wasn't trying to be impressive. She was emptying herself. She wasn't putting on a show. She was pulling on Heaven.

TRAVAIL HITS WHEN YOU HAVE NOTHING LEFT TO MANAGE

You pray tidy prayers when you think you still have options.

Travail shows up when you finally admit you don't.

This is where you let go of timelines, expectations, image, control, and pride. This is when you stop trying to coach God through the process and finally surrender to His authority.

The ugly cry shows up when you're done pretending that you're strong enough to carry this without help.

TRAVAIL BREAKS WHAT SILENCE COULDN'T

There are some things that only break in travail. You've carried the assignment. You've waited. You've been stretched. But now it's time to break through.

Travail breaks what words couldn't.

It's in travail that God starts opening doors, shifting atmospheres, and releasing what's been held up. You're not begging God to do something He forgot. You're partnering with Him to release what's already scheduled.

Romans 8:26 explains this perfectly.

"In the same way, the Ruach (Spirit) helps in our weakness. For we do not know how to pray as we should, but the Ruach Himself intercedes for us with groans too deep for words."

Travail allows the Holy Spirit to take over where your words end.

THE ENEMY FEARS TRAVAIL

The enemy doesn't get nervous when you talk about purpose. He gets nervous when you start travailing for it.

Because travail is violent to Hell's agenda.

Travail shuts down distraction. It exposes lies. It breaks through spiritual resistance. Travail says, "I will not be denied what God has assigned me to carry."

You don't travail for things God never promised. Travail partners with Heaven's plan. That's why it carries so much weight.

THIS IS NOT A DAILY EMOTIONAL MELTDOWN

Let's be clear. Travail is not your weekly breakdown. Travail is not you being dramatic every time something doesn't go your way. Travail is not emotional instability dressed up as spiritual warfare.

Travail is targeted. It's intentional. You are not begging. You are birthing.

True travail requires maturity. You aren't crying because you lost control. You're crying because you've fully surrendered control.

TRAVAIL IS PARTNERSHIP, NOT PERFORMANCE

You don't travail to get God's attention. You already have His attention.

Travail isn't about convincing God to care. It's about aligning yourself with His will at a level your flesh would never choose on its own.

This is why some people avoid travail. It costs too much. It demands full surrender. You can't control the outcome when you travail. You have to trust that God knows what He's delivering through you.

TRAVAIL IS OFTEN PRIVATE

You're not going to have a prayer circle around you every time travail hits. Most of your travail will happen alone, behind closed doors, where nobody sees but God.

That's intentional.

Delivery happens in private before it's announced in public. Travail is where God handles the final spiritual shifts before the release.

AFTER TRAVAIL COMES PEACE

When travail lifts, you'll feel it. The heaviness breaks. The striving stops. The pressure lifts. Not because the promise has fully arrived, but because something has shifted.

The labor is doing its work.

After Hannah travailed, the Bible says, *"Her face was no longer downcast."* (1 Samuel 1:18). That's the peace that comes when you know Heaven has heard you.

PRAYER

Lord, teach me how to partner with You in travail.Strip me of pride, performance, and fear. Bring me into full surrender. I yield my assignment to You completely. Strengthen me to press through until what You have planted is fully released. I trust You to deliver what You've ordained. In Jesus' name, Amen.

REFLECTION QUESTIONS

1. Where have you avoided surrender because you fear the weight of full release?

2. What situations or promises require travail instead of surface-level prayers?

3. How can you make space for private, targeted, Holy Spirit-led travail?

Chapter 13
PUSH: PRAY UNTIL SOMETHING HAPPENS (AND KEEP PRAYING AFTER IT DOES)

This is where everybody loves to shout.

"PUSH!" "Pray until something happens!" It sounds so powerful when you say it out loud. They put it on t-shirts. They post it on social media. They turn it into hashtags.

But here's the part they don't say.

PUSH isn't stylish. PUSH isn't polished. PUSH is exhausting. PUSH is ugly. PUSH will have you sweating in prayer while everyone else is still waiting for a praise report to post.

The reason most people stop short is because they didn't realize what pushing would cost.

PUSHING TAKES MORE THAN A PRAYER

When people say, "just pray," they make it sound like this is easy work.

You pray and God just drops the promise in your lap like Amazon Prime.

PUSH requires stamina. This isn't a one-time prayer you squeeze in before dinner. PUSH is consistency when nothing looks like it's moving. PUSH is getting up again after you've already worn yourself out emotionally.

It's easy to pray for what you want. It takes maturity to keep praying when you don't know when it's coming.

PUSH IS MENTAL

Before it's physical, before you see any evidence, PUSH starts in your head. This is where the warfare intensifies.

You'll start questioning whether your prayers are even working.

The enemy will throw every distraction possible to make you think you're wasting your time.

He wants you to believe that silence equals failure.

The mental fight is often heavier than the spiritual one. You don't just have to stay on your knees. You have to stay in your mind.

PUSH ISN'T A RELIGIOUS PERFORMANCE

You don't PUSH so people can watch you pray. You PUSH because you refuse to leave the delivery room empty-handed.

This isn't the kind of praying where you're making sure your volume is impressive. This isn't you performing for the people sitting around you at the altar.

You can whisper or shout. You can cry or sit silent. None of that moves Heaven. What moves Heaven is your endurance in prayer. Your refusal to let go of what God already said.

PUSH ISN'T ALWAYS PRETTY

Some people think that if they're really anointed, they should be able to PUSH gracefully.

Nope.

Sometimes you're going to be anointed and exhausted at the same time. You will pray and still cry. You will pray and still feel overwhelmed. You will pray and still want to quit.

That's normal. You're not less spiritual. You're not weak. You're in labor.

Labor isn't about how you look while you push. It's about what comes forth because you didn't quit.

PUSH DOESN'T GUARANTEE SPEED

Let's talk about one of the most disappointing moments in this process.

You finally feel the shift. You finally feel like God is moving. You PUSH in prayer expecting immediate delivery. Then nothing happens.

You assume something went wrong. But sometimes God allows the PUSH to continue even after the first breakthrough hits. Because the assignment isn't small. It requires sustained intercession.

Just because you feel the head doesn't mean the body has been delivered yet. The work isn't finished until the full promise comes forth.

PUSH REQUIRES PARTNERS

Nobody pushes well in isolation.

In natural labor, there's a whole team present. Nurses. Midwives. Doctors. Coaches. Nobody looks at a woman in labor and says, "Figure it out by yourself."

The same applies spiritually. You need people around you who know how to pray when you get tired. People who know how to cover you when your emotions are unstable. People who aren't intimidated by your contractions.

You need people who will grab your hand and say, "I know you're tired. But you're not leaving this room empty."

PUSH CONTINUES EVEN AFTER DELIVERY

Here's where a lot of people drop the ball. They think PUSH stops once the promise shows up.

Wrong.

PUSH continues long after delivery. Now you have to pray to protect what was delivered. You pray over the assignment. You pray over your stewardship. You pray over your obedience moving forward.

The enemy doesn't stop after delivery. If anything, he ramps up because now there's something visible to attack.

Your prayer life doesn't end at delivery. It shifts into a new dimension.

THIS IS WHERE THE REAL FIGHT HAPPENS

If you're going to carry purpose, you better know how to PUSH.

You can't afford to be lazy in prayer. You can't afford to be passive in the Spirit. You can't afford to treat prayer like a checkbox.

PUSH is how you survive carrying what God has assigned.

It's not hype. It's survival.

PRAYER

Lord, strengthen me to PUSH until the assignment is fully delivered. Give me stamina in prayer. Guard my mind when discouragement tries to steal my endurance. Surround me with people who will cover me in prayer. Teach me how to press even when I feel empty. I will not leave this process without

*delivering what You have planted in me. In Jesus'
name, Amen.*

REFLECTION QUESTIONS

1. Where have you grown weary in prayer while carrying your assignment?

2. Who do you have around you to help you PUSH when you get tired?

3. What can you do to strengthen your prayer life as you continue pressing toward delivery?

Chapter 14

MIDWIVES AND MONSTERS: DISCERNMENT IN YOUR DELIVERY ROOM

When you're getting ready to deliver what God has placed inside you, you don't just need people. You need the right people.

Not everyone qualified to sit at your table is qualified to stand at your bedside.

When labor hits, your circle matters more than your gift. Because the wrong people in your delivery room don't just slow you down. They threaten what you're about to release.

EVERYONE CHEERS CONCEPTION. NOT EVERY-ONE STAYS FOR DELIVERY.

When you first start sharing your God-given assignment, everybody's excited.

"Girl, I'm so proud of you!" "You're doing big things!" "I'm praying for you!"

They love the idea of what you're carrying. But the closer you get to delivery, the thinner the crowd becomes. The excitement wears off when the work gets heavy, when the warfare increases, and when your full obedience starts exposing their partial obedience.

This is why you cannot confuse fans with midwives.

MIDWIVES KNOW HOW TO HANDLE PAIN WITHOUT PANIC

A true midwife can handle you at your worst moment without flinching.

You might be moaning. You might be exhausted. You might say things you don't even mean because the pressure has you emotional. A real midwife doesn't take it personal. She stays steady. She stays focused. She reminds you why you started. She knows when to tell you to rest and when to tell you to PUSH.

This is not a friend who just likes posting selfies with you. This is someone assigned to your assignment.

Exodus 1 gives us a powerful picture. Pharaoh commanded the Hebrew midwives to kill every son born to the Israelites. But the midwives feared God and protected the babies (Exodus 1:15-17).

That's what real midwives do. They protect what God is birthing, even when it's risky to stand with you.

MONSTERS SHOW UP WHEN IT'S TIME TO DELIVER

Let's deal with the other side.

There are some people who cannot handle you delivering what God put inside you.

Some of them won't say it outright. They'll just start acting funny. The support fades. The calls slow down. The little side comments start dropping. You can feel their energy shift.

Others are bolder. They'll question your timing. They'll challenge your decisions. They'll remind you of your weaknesses. They'll try to insert fear, doubt, and confusion right when you're most vulnerable.

Their goal isn't always to destroy you. Sometimes they just want to delay you long enough that you abandon the assignment.

SOME PEOPLE WERE COMFORTABLE WITH YOUR BARREN SEASON

It's not always jealousy over your success. Sometimes people were simply more comfortable with you before you stepped into obedience.

Your faith forces them to confront their compromise. Your boldness exposes their fear. Your obedience makes them uncomfortable with how long they've been disobedient.

It's easier for them if you stay where you were. That way, nobody has to face their own assignment.

MONSTERS AREN'T ALWAYS OBVIOUS

Some of the people you need to guard against don't come in loud and messy.

They come polite. They sound wise. They use churchy language.

"It's just a lot right now. Maybe you should slow down and make sure you're hearing God." "Are you sure this is the right season? Timing is everything." "Don't you think you should wait for more confirmation?"

Translation: they don't have the faith to match your delivery, so they're projecting their fear onto your assignment.

YOU'RE NOT BEING RUDE. YOU'RE BEING RESPONSIBLE.

Let me settle this for you right now.

You don't owe anyone access to your delivery room. You don't need to explain who gets to stay.You don't need to justify why certain people no longer have the same level of access.

Your job isn't to comfort people's egos. Your job is to protect the promise.

DISCERNMENT SAVES DELIVERIES

Discernment is not about reading vibes. Discernment is hearing the Holy Spirit say, "This one can stay. That one cannot."

Think about Gideon for a minute. He started with 32,000 men ready to go into battle. God trimmed it all the way down to 300 (Judges 7). Not because the others weren't willing, but because they weren't equipped for the level of victory God was about to release.

Your delivery room works the same way. God will thin the crowd, not to punish you, but to protect what He's birthing through you. The fewer people in the room, the less room for fear, doubt, or distraction to creep in.

EVERY MIDWIFE MUST BE ASSIGNED, NOT SELECTED

Stop handpicking people based on loyalty, history, or who's been around the longest. Length of friendship does not equal capacity for this assignment.

Some people you've known forever still can't handle where you're going. And that's okay. But don't mistake loyalty for assignment.

Let God assign your midwives. The people He sends will carry your contractions in prayer, not your business in gossip.

PRAYER

Lord, sharpen my discernment as I approach delivery.Show me who belongs in my birthing room. Remove every voice that would introduce fear, doubt, or distraction. Surround me with people who carry Your heart and who can handle my process. I release every relationship You have not assigned to this season. I trust You to protect both the promise and the room.In Jesus' name, Amen.

REFLECTION QUESTIONS

1. Who in your life carries the faith to stand with you during delivery?

2. What relationships feel strained as you move deeper into your assignment?

3. Where do you need to set boundaries to protect your birthing room?

Chapter 15
BIRTHING TIME: GOD OPENS WHAT YOU CAN'T

You've carried. You've waited. You've prayed. You've been stretched. You've travailed.You've pushed.

Now comes the moment that separates what you can control from what only God can do.

Because no matter how much preparation you've done, **you don't open your own womb.**

DELIVERY REQUIRES DIVINE OPENING

In natural labor, you can push all you want, but until the body opens, the baby doesn't come.

Spiritually, it's no different. You don't force your way into release. You can't manipulate God's schedule. The opening belongs to Him.

Genesis 30:22 says it plainly:

"Then God remembered Rachel. God listened to her and opened her womb."

Rachel couldn't open her own womb. Neither can you.

Your job was never to break open the door. Your job was to stay positioned long enough for God to open it.

YOU DON'T DELIVER BY HUSTLING HARDER

This is where a lot of people start messing things up. They feel the contractions. They sense the timing is close. So, they panic.

Instead of staying steady, they start forcing doors open.

They network themselves into rooms they were never invited into. They launch assignments that aren't fully ready. They chase visibility instead of authority. They confuse busy with birthing.

The delivery happens when God opens what your effort never could.

SOMETIMES GOD MAKES YOU WAIT UNTIL THE ROOM IS READY

The womb isn't the only thing God's opening.

He's opening the room you're about to walk into. The people who need to hear your voice. The territory assigned to your gift. The platforms attached to your purpose.

He's not stalling you. He's preparing your landing place.

If you deliver too soon, you'll walk into a room that wasn't ready to receive you. That's how burnout happens. That's how frustration builds. That's how assignments collapse.

When God opens it, it's fully prepared for what you're carrying.

YOU'RE NOT RESPONSIBLE FOR WHO SEES IT

One of the hardest parts about birthing time is letting go of who shows up for it.

Some people you thought would be there won't be. Some people who doubted you will be forced to watch. Some people you didn't expect will show up out of nowhere.

The crowd is not your concern. The audience doesn't control the outcome. Delivery belongs to God.

Isaiah 43:19 reminds us:

> *"Behold, I am doing a new thing. Now it is spring-*
> *ing up. Do you not know about it? I will surely make*
> *a way in the desert, rivers in the wasteland."*

He doesn't need anyone's permission to make room for you.

WHAT GOD OPENS, NO ONE CAN CLOSE

When God opens a door, no enemy can shut it. No sabotage can block it. No jealousy can undo it. No opinion can reverse it.

Revelation 3:8 says it perfectly:

> *"See, I have set before you an open door that no one*
> *is able to shut."*

That's the confidence you stand in when birthing time arrives. You're not trying to maintain it in your own strength. What God has opened, He will sustain.

DELIVERY REQUIRES RELEASE

Here's the part that stings.

Birthing time means you have to let it go. You've carried this assignment for so long, it almost feels safer to hold it than to release it.

But you can't carry what's full-term forever. Holding onto something that's ready to be delivered becomes disobedience, not stewardship.

You prepared for this. Now you have to trust God enough to release it into the world.

DELIVERY IS PUBLIC, BUT DEVELOPMENT WAS PRIVATE

For months, nobody saw what was growing.

They didn't see your private obedience. They didn't see your quiet sacrifice. They didn't see the late-night tears, the whispered prayers, the warfare behind the scenes.

But when God delivers, the fruit becomes public. Not to showcase you, but to showcase His faithfulness.

That's why you don't have to worry about promoting yourself. Delivery becomes its own announcement.

THE DOOR YOU COULDN'T OPEN IS NOW OPEN

You didn't manipulate it. You didn't market your way into it. You didn't hustle to create it.

You waited. You obeyed. You trusted. And now the door has opened.

You are not standing here because of your brilliance. You are standing here because God opened what you couldn't.

PRAYER

Lord, I trust You to open every door in Your timing. I release my grip on what I've carried. I surrender my fear of release. Open the places that are assigned to my purpose. Prepare every room You've called me into.Protect what I deliver as it enters into the world. I will not strive to maintain what You've ordained.In Jesus' name, Amen.

REFLECTION QUESTIONS

1. Where have you tried to force doors open instead of waiting for God's timing?

2. What fears do you feel about releasing your assignment publicly?

3. How can you stay anchored as God opens doors you couldn't create for yourself?

Chapter 16
POSTPARTUM PURPOSE: DON'T DROP WHAT YOU JUST DELIVERED

You finally delivered. You prayed, pushed, travailed, fought hell, cried in the car, threatened to quit at least seventeen times, and somehow made it to the other side.

The promise is here. The assignment is visible. The fruit is undeniable. And if we're being real, you're officially too tired to celebrate like you thought you would. You thought you'd be shouting in the aisles. Instead, you're quietly wondering if you can take a nap before anyone asks you for anything else.

Because nobody told you that birthing purpose was only step one. The real work starts now.

DELIVERY IS LOUD. STEWARDSHIP IS QUIET

Delivery gets all the attention.

People love balloons. They love an announcement post. They'll double tap your testimony and tag themselves in your victory like they were there in the trenches with you.

Stewardship? That's not as glamorous. That's you, your assignment, and a whole lot of coffee at 2am while everyone else sleeps. That's the unseen part where the work gets real and the applause gets quiet.

You're not in delivery anymore. Now you're in maintenance. And maintenance isn't sexy, but it's holy.

THE ENEMY KNOWS WHEN TO CHANGE STRATEGIES

The enemy didn't stop just because the delivery came through. He simply updated his playbook.

He knows he couldn't block what you birthed. So now he'll attack your consistency. If he can't stop you from delivering it, he'll try to drain you into neglecting it.

Look at Solomon. Started strong. Full of wisdom. Overflowing with God's favor. But somewhere along the way, distractions crept in. He started compromising his stewardship, and eventually, the kingdom slipped (1 Kings 11).

Solomon didn't fall because he wasn't called. He fell because he mismanaged what he was trusted to carry.

THE BLESSING STILL REQUIRES BOUNDARIES

Don't let your own success trick you into dropping your guard.

The assignment may be birthed, but it still needs protection. Time boundaries. Emotional boundaries. Financial boundaries. Spiritual boundaries.

Every new promise invites new distractions. Every new platform invites new pressures. You don't protect your purpose one time. You protect it every day.

THE WEIGHT FEELS DIFFERENT AFTER DELIVERY

Waiting was one kind of weight. This is another.

Before delivery, you were carrying expectation.Now you're carrying responsibility.

And let's be honest, there's a moment where you look at what you prayed for, and you silently think, "Whew. This is heavier than I pictured when I was journaling about it."

That's growth. God didn't call you to carry something small. He trusted you with something that requires full-grown spiritual strength.

PURPOSE FATIGUE IS REAL

The adrenaline of delivery fades fast. And once it's gone, the temptation creeps in:

"Maybe I just need a little break from this calling."

Translation? "I wonder if God would be okay if I just took a six-month vacation from obedience."

That's not a sabbatical, sis. That's how assignments get messy. You don't take extended vacations from something God trusted you to lead. You steward it. You stay accountable to it.

Fatigue isn't fixed by walking away from the promise. It's fixed by staying connected to the One who gave it.

STAYING FED KEEPS YOU FROM STARVING THE PROMISE

You cannot lead an assignment while running on spiritual fumes.

When you delivered, you got attention. Now that you're stewarding, you need fuel.

Look at Jesus in John 21. After the resurrection, He didn't send His disciples right into ministry burnout. He made them breakfast. He fed them before He commissioned them. Even Jesus knew: you can't assign people who haven't eaten.

Keep yourself fed in prayer. In the Word. In wise counsel. Don't let spiritual malnourishment kill what you fought to birth.

DON'T ROMANTICIZE THE NEXT ASSIGNMENT TO ESCAPE THIS ONE

Here comes the shiny temptation.

A new idea shows up. A new opportunity appears. And suddenly, what you just delivered doesn't feel as exciting anymore. Guess how I know this!

The next thing always looks better from a distance. The same way toddlers look angelic when they're asleep, until they wake up and you remember why you needed coffee. Same with new assignments.

Don't run from your current responsibility chasing something new you aren't even ready for yet.

THE PROMISE WAS NEVER SUPPOSED TO SELF-MAINTAIN

God birthed it through you. But He never intended for you to maintain it by yourself.

The same grace that carried you through labor is the grace that will sustain you through stewardship. But you have to stay surrendered. You have to stay disciplined. You have to stay close.

You are not maintaining this in your own strength. You're managing what God trusted you to lead. And He never asked you to do that without Him.

PRAYER

Lord, strengthen me to steward what I've delivered. Guard me from fatigue, distraction, and compromise. Help me stay disciplined and faithful. Keep my ears sensitive to Your voice as I lead what You've placed in my hands I will not drop what You trusted me to carry. In Jesus' name, Amen.

REFLECTION QUESTIONS

1. Where have you felt fatigue or discouragement since delivering your assignment?

2. What areas of stewardship require more intentional discipline?

3. How can you create space to stay spiritually fed as you lead this promise?

Chapter 17
STEWARDSHIP OVER STATUS: THE WORK AFTER THE APPLAUSE

The applause feels good, doesn't it?

Let's not pretend it doesn't. You fought for this. You sacrificed for this. You spent plenty of nights wondering if you were crazy for believing God would do it. And now that He has, the congratulations start rolling in.

You finally got the platform. The speaking invitations are coming. The social media numbers are climbing. People are quoting you now. Your name is getting mentioned in rooms you prayed to enter.

That applause feels like confirmation. But here's the part most people miss.

The applause is not your assignment. The stewardship is.

APPLAUSE IS SHORT. STEWARDSHIP IS LONG.

The problem isn't the applause. The problem is what happens when you start needing it.

Applause is loud in the beginning. But it fades. People move on. Their attention shifts. The same people who screamed "you're amazing" last month are busy watching somebody else this month.

If you don't have your identity rooted in God's assignment, you'll start chasing claps instead of carrying purpose.

You were never called to maintain public approval. You were called to manage God's assignment.

THE CROWD WILL TRY TO PROMOTE YOU PAST YOUR ASSIGNMENT

Be careful. Because not every opportunity that shows up after delivery is God's elevation.

Some of it is human promotion disguised as divine favor. They'll tell you, "You should be doing more." "You should write another book...right now." "You should go full-time ministry tomorrow."

"You should take this speaking opportunity, even though it's not your lane."

What they're really doing is trying to elevate your status faster than God has built your foundation. And rushed elevation leads to unstable leadership.

JESUS REPEATEDLY WALKED AWAY FROM THE CROWD

Let's be really clear. Jesus had no shortage of fans. The crowds followed Him everywhere. But He was never addicted to their attention.

When they tried to force Him into premature promotion, He walked away. When they praised Him for the miracles, He withdrew to pray. (Luke 5:15-16)

He was never moved by the size of the crowd. He stayed focused on the Father's assignment.

That's your model.

STATUS DOESN'T SUSTAIN PURPOSE

You can get the platform and still lose the presence. You can gain followers and still lose your footing. You can build the brand and still lose the oil.

If you start managing your assignment based on what keeps you popular, you will eventually compromise what keeps you anointed.

Popularity is not always evidence of God's approval. Obedience is.

THE PRESSURE TO PRODUCE NEVER STOPS

Once the applause comes, you'll feel it.

The pressure to outdo your last success. The temptation to keep feeding people new content so you stay relevant. The subtle fear that if you don't stay visible, you'll lose momentum.

And if you give in to that pressure, you'll start producing things God never assigned just to keep the applause going. That's how people end up burned out, drained, and performing for platforms they were never supposed to be on.

YOU DON'T NEED TO PROVE WHAT GOD ALREADY PROMOTED

Listen carefully.

If God promoted you, you don't need to perform to prove you deserve to be there. The open door was His responsibility. The obedience inside the door is yours.

You don't have to match anyone's pace. You don't have to chase anyone's formula. You don't have to create pressure where God gave peace.

When you steward well, God sustains what He started.

STAY GROUNDED OR YOU'LL GET DRUNK ON APPLAUSE

Applause is addictive. The danger isn't the sound itself. The danger is when you start drinking it.

It feels good when people recognize you. When they start calling you "anointed" and "powerful" and "so gifted."

But if you don't stay grounded, you'll start believing your own press releases instead of staying dependent on God's voice. That's how assignments shift from holy to hollow.

Stay sober.

STEWARDSHIP IS QUIET, CONSISTENT WORK

Stewardship doesn't need a stage. Stewardship happens in your prayer closet, not your comment section. Stewardship is studying when nobody's watching. It's managing your assignment when nobody's tagging you. It's staying accountable even when no one's checking.

Stewardship will keep you where applause can't.

Luke 16:10 says:

> *"Whoever is faithful in the smallest is also faithful in much." God promotes based on stewardship, not status.*

PRAYER

Lord, keep my heart anchored in You, not in applause. Help me steward my assignment with faithfulness, even when no one is watching. Protect me from the temptation to chase status or public approval. Remind me that You are my promoter, my sus-

tainer, and my source. I will not compromise my obedience for attention. I will steward what You've given me with integrity.In Jesus' name, Amen.

REFLECTION QUESTIONS

1. Where have you felt the pressure to maintain applause or stay visible?

2. Are there opportunities in front of you that are tempting but not assigned?

3. How can you protect your heart from status addiction and stay rooted in stewardship?

Chapter 18

DELIVERY ROOM DEBRIEF: WHAT GOD WAS REALLY DOING IN YOU

Now that you've delivered, let's sit down for a minute and chat.

Because while you've been so focused on what you were carrying, you may have missed what God was doing in you while you carried it.

See, you thought this whole process was about the assignment. And it was...partly. But the bigger work wasn't happening in your hands. It was happening in your heart.

THE ASSIGNMENT WAS NEVER JUST ABOUT THE ASSIGNMENT

Yes, God called you to deliver something. Yes, He put purpose inside of you. But this process wasn't just about birthing a ministry, a business, a book, or whatever your assignment looks like.

This was about making you into the kind of person who could steward what He put in your hands.

You were the first construction site. The assignment was never going to be healthy if you stayed unhealthy. The promise was never going to flourish if you were still functioning in fear, pride, insecurity, or control.

God wasn't just building your platform. He was building your character.

YOUR CAPACITY HAD TO GROW BEFORE YOUR INFLUENCE COULD

There were things God had to stretch in you before He could release the influence through you.

You thought you were ready when you first prayed for the promise. You weren't. And that's not an insult. That's protection.

If God had opened the doors back then, you would've mishandled what's now in your hands. Not because you didn't love Him. Not because you weren't sincere. But because you didn't yet have the capacity to carry the weight that came with it.

Growth isn't punishment. Growth is preparation.

HE BURNED OUT YOUR DEPENDENCE ON PEOPLE

Remember when you used to need everybody's approval? Remember how you used to get rattled when people didn't support you? Remember how much you depended on outside validation to feel like you were making progress?

That version of you didn't survive the process. God let you walk through the silence, the loneliness, the stripped-down seasons, so that when the promise finally came, your confidence was rooted in Him, not in who was clapping for you.

THE SILENCE WAS TRAINING YOU TO HEAR HIS VOICE ALONE

You learned how to stand when nobody was confirming you.

You learned how to pray without a choir cheering you on. You learned how to obey when it felt like God was quiet. You learned how to stay planted even when everything in you wanted to run.

That was never wasted time. That was discipline being built into your spirit.

YOU STOPPED TRYING TO CONTROL THE TIMING

One of the biggest miracles wasn't just what He birthed, it's that you finally surrendered your obsession with when it would happen.

You stopped trying to bargain with God.You stopped trying to manufacture open doors. You stopped trying to prove you were ready before He said you were.

The release came after the surrender, not before.

YOU LEARNED TO LET PEOPLE LEAVE

You discovered that not everyone could walk with you through the whole process. And more importantly, you learned how to let them go without falling apart.

You stopped trying to drag people who weren't assigned. You stopped chasing approval from people who couldn't understand your process. You stopped apologizing for your obedience.

That level of release was part of your development.

YOU BUILT SPIRITUAL ENDURANCE

You're not easily rattled anymore. You don't fall apart like you used to. Because you've been through real labor. You know what it feels like to want to quit but keep pushing. You know what it feels like to be exhausted but stay obedient. You know what it feels like to carry something long past your comfort zone.

That endurance didn't come from books or conferences. It came from the pressure that forced you to trust God for real.

THE ASSIGNMENT GREW. BUT SO DID YOU.

The real victory isn't just that you delivered what God put in you. It's that He delivered something in you.

Confidence. Maturity. Strength. Discipline. Stability. Peace. Authority.

You don't sound like you used to. You don't think like you used to. You don't respond like you used to. You've been changed by the process.

THIS WAS NEVER JUST ABOUT WHAT YOU COULD DO

God wasn't using you to get a project done. He was using the assignment to shape you into the woman He created you to be.

You didn't just birth the promise. The promise birthed you.

PRAYER

Lord, thank You for what You've done in me through this process. I see now that You were working on my heart even while I was carrying the assignment. Thank You for stripping away pride, fear, and dependence on others. Thank You for growing my capacity, my confidence, and my endurance. Continue to shape me as I steward what You've delivered. In Jesus' name, Amen.

REFLECTION QUESTIONS

1. How have you personally grown through the process of carrying and delivering your assignment?

2. What areas of your life did God transform while you were waiting?

3. How can you continue to stay surrendered as He shapes you for what's next?

Chapter 19
THE RECOVERY ROOM: RESTING WITHOUT ABANDONING THE ASSIGNMENT

You made it. The promise is here. You pushed, travailed, fought, prayed, cried, and survived what most people don't even have language for.

Now you're exhausted. And you know what? That's not a spiritual failure. That's called being human.

Delivering an assignment takes something out of you. You didn't imagine how heavy this would feel. You didn't exaggerate how drained you are right now. This is the part nobody preaches about because it's not exciting enough for the conference flyer.

Welcome to the recovery room.

DELIVERY TAKES EVERYTHING OUT OF YOU

Labor doesn't just drain you physically. It drains you spiritually. It drains you emotionally. You've spent months, even years, carrying weight that most people couldn't see. Now that it's out, you feel emptied in every possible way.

You're not broken. You're not weak. You're not unspiritual. You're just poured out.

This is the place where God doesn't ask you to perform. He invites you to breathe.

REST IS NOT RETREAT

Let's get one thing straight. Rest is not quitting. Rest is not abandoning the assignment. Rest is not throwing your hands up and walking away because you feel overwhelmed.

Rest is a divine pause. God gives you permission to step back and let Him refill what the process drained. You're not neglecting the promise. You're making sure you're strong enough to carry it long-term.

Quitting says, "I can't do this."Rest says, "Let me catch my breath so I can keep doing this."

You're not failing because you need a moment. You're protecting what God gave you.

JESUS KNEW HOW TO SIT DOWN

Don't over-spiritualize yourself into burnout. Jesus Himself didn't run nonstop.

In Mark 6, after ministering to crowds and feeding thousands, Jesus told His disciples:

> *"Come away by yourselves to an isolated place and rest a while."*

He wasn't giving a suggestion. He was giving a survival strategy.

If the Son of God can say, "I need a minute," you can too.

You don't earn extra crowns for running yourself into the ground in the name of ministry.

THE PRESSURE TO "KEEP PRODUCING" IS A TRAP

The moment you deliver, the world starts expecting your next move.

People will ask, "What's next?" like you're supposed to have five more projects lined up.

They will cheer you into premature production if you let them.

Don't fall for it. Delivering purpose isn't about staying busy. It's about staying obedient. If God hasn't assigned something new, sit yourself down and enjoy the season He has you in.

REST PROTECTS THE PROMISE

Exhaustion makes you sloppy. It makes you careless. It makes you vulnerable.

That's why the enemy loves to push high performers into burnout. If he can't stop your obedience, he'll try to drain your stamina until you start compromising what you delivered.

Rest keeps your judgment clear. It keeps your emotions stable. It keeps your discernment sharp. You don't lead well when you're fried. You lead well when you're rested.

GOD ISN'T IMPRESSED BY YOUR HUSTLE

We love to confuse activity with obedience. We assume that if we're constantly doing something, we must be pleasing God.

But God is not impressed by your busy calendar. He is not moved by how many events you book, how many posts you schedule, or how many projects you launch.

What moves God is your surrender. Sometimes surrender sounds like, "I need to sit down for a second." And God is perfectly fine with that.

REST IS PART OF THE ASSIGNMENT

You don't rest because you're lazy. You rest because you're strategic.

You can't carry what God gave you long-term if you refuse to let Him refuel you. You're not useful to anyone if you're leading on fumes.

The recovery room isn't wasted time. It's how you make sure you don't collapse under the very thing you fought to deliver.

PRAYER

Lord, I give myself permission to rest. I trust You to refresh what has been poured out. Keep me from performance and striving. Teach me how to recover without abandoning what You've assigned.Refill my strength so I can carry what You've delivered through me. In Jesus' name, Amen.

REFLECTION QUESTIONS

1. Where have you confused rest with disobedience or quitting?

2. How has fatigue affected your ability to steward the promise?

3. What practical steps can you take to create intentional recovery time?

Chapter 20
THE AFTERBIRTH: DEALING WITH WHAT GETS LEFT BEHIND

Everyone loves to celebrate the baby.

They're oohing and ahhing over what you just delivered. They're posting it. They're praising it. They're calling it "beautiful."

Nobody's talking about the afterbirth.

You know. The part that gets left behind once delivery happens. The part that nobody wants to see on Instagram. The part that's necessary but messy.

The afterbirth isn't the promise. But you still have to deal with it.

JUST BECAUSE IT CAME OUT WITH THE PROMISE DOESN'T MEAN IT'S PART OF THE PROMISE

The afterbirth served a purpose while you were carrying. It nourished the assignment. It protected what was growing. But now that the promise is delivered, its job is done.

If you try to keep what God designed to be temporary, you'll end up dragging unnecessary weight into your next season.

You can't keep everything that was part of your carrying season. Some things were only assigned to sustain you while you were pregnant. Now it's time to release them.

THE ATTACHMENTS THAT HELPED YOU THEN CAN HURT YOU NOW

Let's make it real.

There were habits, people, coping mechanisms, and routines that helped you survive the pressure of carrying purpose. They were like spiritual crutches while you were under weight.

But you don't need crutches when you're walking in fulfillment. You can't keep leaning on survival strategies that don't fit your delivered season.

You needed that prayer circle to hold you up while you were fighting warfare at 2am. Now God's calling you to stand with the authority you gained through that very warfare.

You needed those tight boundaries to protect your fragile yes. Now God may call you to stretch those boundaries as you lead.

You needed that private space of hiding while He was developing you. Now He's calling you to step into visibility with stability.

Don't mistake temporary scaffolding for permanent structure.

EMOTIONAL ATTACHMENTS ARE THE HARDEST PART TO CUT

Let's not act brand new.

Some of what God is telling you to release, you actually liked.

You liked how certain people made you feel important when you were doubting yourself. You liked having a small circle where you didn't have to risk exposure. You liked staying under the radar where nobody could critique what you hadn't delivered yet.

But now the promise is here. And the comfort zone you enjoyed while carrying it will suffocate you if you refuse to release what no longer serves your assignment.

AFTERBIRTH LEFT UNADDRESSED BECOMES A THREAT

In the natural, if the afterbirth doesn't pass fully, it can become toxic. It can cause infection. It can threaten the health of both the mother and the child.

Spiritually, the same is true.

When you refuse to release what God is trying to clear out, you create space for bitterness, insecurity, resentment, and pride to infect your new season.

What once served you will eventually poison you if you refuse to let it go.

THE RELEASE IS ABOUT ALIGNMENT, NOT USING PEOPLE

Sometimes releasing certain people or habits makes you feel guilty.

You start thinking: "But they were there for me." "But they helped me when I was struggling." "But I owe them." "Doing that always worked for me in the past."

Let's be really clear here.

This isn't about using people for what they gave you and then cutting them off like they're disposable. That's not kingdom, that's foolishness.

This is not "thank you for getting me here, now you're dead weight." This is about roles, not relationship. This is about understanding that every person plays a role for a season. Some are assigned for the long haul. Others were assigned to hold space during the formation season.

Honoring what someone contributed doesn't mean you drag them where God never assigned them to go. That would not be fair to them and their assignment either. Their role may have been necessary in your becoming, but that doesn't mean they are called to walk with you into every new dimension of your assignment.

It's not cutting people loose because they're inconvenient. It's releasing people from roles when God shifts your season, and your assignments no longer align.

YOU CAN GRIEVE AND RELEASE AT THE SAME TIME

It's okay to feel sad while God removes things from your life. You're not weak because you feel the sting of release. That grief is normal. It just can't lead you.

God is not asking you to pretend you're fine. He's asking you to trust that what He's removing was never designed to stay.

DON'T TAKE LEFTOVER BAGGAGE INTO YOUR NEW SEASON

The assignment is delivered. The work continues. But don't sabotage your next by clinging to leftovers from your last.

Clean hands make room for full stewardship. You're not losing. You're clearing space.

PRAYER

Lord, help me release everything You have not assigned to s tay.Show me what was only meant for the carrying season. Break emotional attachments that make me hesitant to obey. I trust You to remove what I no longer need so I can steward this assignment in freedom. In Jesus' name, Amen.

REFLECTION QUESTIONS

1. What habits, relationships, or patterns served you during the carrying season but need to be released now?

2. Where have you hesitated to release what God is clearly calling you to let go?

3. How can you embrace release as part of obedience and preparation for what's next?

Chapter 21
YOU DELIVERED: NOW RAISE IT

Delivery felt like the goal. That's what you prayed for. That's what you fought for. That's what everyone was shouting about when you finally pushed through.

And now the assignment is out in the open.

But here's the part nobody tells you at the conference. Delivering the promise was not the finish line. It was the starting point.

You didn't just birth something. You gave life to something that has to be raised.

DELIVERING PURPOSE IS EXCITING. RAISING PURPOSE IS WORK.

When you first deliver, everybody wants to hold the baby. They're clapping, posting, cheering, and congratulating you for finally birthing what God promised.

But once the celebration fades, you're left with the part no one wants to post about. The daily work of raising what you delivered.

You have to feed it. You have to protect it. You have to grow it. You have to discipline it. You have to manage it.

This is where purpose shifts from emotional to practical. You don't get to coast now. You have to lead what you labored for.

BABIES DON'T RAISE THEMSELVES

In the natural, no one would hand you a newborn and say, "Well, congrats. You did it. Good luck."

We all know that birth is beautiful, but the real work starts after you leave the hospital. The baby has to be nurtured, trained, disciplined, and grown into maturity.

Your assignment is no different.

If you don't raise it, you will drop it. If you drop it, someone else may pick it up, but not with the grace or authority God originally assigned to you.

You can't delegate raising what God entrusted you to carry.

RAISING THE ASSIGNMENT REQUIRES DIFFER-ENT SKILLS

Carrying it required patience. Delivering it required surrender. Raising it requires stewardship.

You now have to lead meetings. Set structure. Manage resources. Handle people. Make hard decisions. Keep your motives clean.

This is where many people fail because they thought the gift would carry itself. The gift is powerful, but the leadership around the gift matters just as much.

YOU WILL BE TEMPTED TO SPOIL WHAT YOU DELIVERED

Now here's where it gets personal.

You prayed so long for this assignment that when it finally arrived, you became overly protective. You don't want anyone correcting it. You don't want to make adjustments. You don't want to change anything that makes you uncomfortable.

You start babying what God is calling you to build.

A spoiled assignment doesn't grow. It stays immature. It stays dependent. It stays small because you refuse to challenge it.

You can't lead something you're afraid to develop. Love it enough to grow it.

RAISING YOUR ASSIGNMENT WILL COST YOU AGAIN

Delivery was one sacrifice. Raising it will require another.

You will have to give up comfort to maintain consistency. You will have to fight distraction to stay focused. You will have to protect your personal time with God so your private life doesn't collapse under your public platform.

The enemy can't steal what you delivered, but he will attack how you manage it. Your stewardship is how you defend the promise.

YOU WILL NEED NEW COUNSEL IN THIS SEASON

The people who coached you through carrying may not be the ones who coach you through raising.

Don't confuse familiarity with capacity. Raising requires wisdom from people who understand leadership, growth, and maturity. You don't need cheerleaders right now. You need wise counsel who can call you out, build you up, and hold you accountable.

GOD DOESN'T JUST WANT IT BORN. HE WANTS IT BUILT

You didn't go through all of that labor just to birth something pretty. God wants fruit that remains.

John 15:16 says:

> *"You did not choose Me, but I chose you. I appointed*
> *you to go and produce fruit that will last."*

Your job now is not simply to display the assignment but to develop it into what God intended.

PRAYER

Lord, teach me how to raise what You've delivered through me.Give me wisdom, discipline, and endurance. Surround me with counsel that helps me grow in leadership. Keep my heart humble as I steward this assignment. I will not neglect what I've carried. I will not drop what You trusted me to raise.In Jesus' name, Amen.

REFLECTION QUESTIONS

1. Where have you been tempted to stop leading and start coasting after delivery?

2. What areas of your assignment need stronger structure or leadership?

3. Who do you need in your life to help you steward this assignment in its next stage?

Chapter 22
THE MULTIPLICATION: THE PROMISE WAS NEVER JUST ABOUT YOU

You thought this was about you.

It felt personal because you were carrying it. You were the one crying. You were the one praying. You were the one pushing. You were the one fighting the warfare.

But now you're starting to see what God knew from the start. This was never just about your blessing. This was about multiplication.

GOD NEVER DELIVERS PURPOSE JUST FOR ONE PERSON

You carried it, but it was never meant to stop with you.

Every God-assigned purpose carries ripple effects. Somebody else's breakthrough is attached to your obedience. Somebody else's deliverance is sitting on the other side of your yes.

You weren't just birthing for your comfort. You were birthing for kingdom impact. And if you try to shrink your assignment down to personal convenience, you will cheat the people God assigned to your fruit.

MULTIPLICATION REQUIRES YOU TO LET GO OF CONTROL

Here's where it gets uncomfortable.

You've been protecting what you birthed. You've been raising it carefully. You've been stewarding it with discipline. But now God is expanding it. And expansion requires release.

You can't micromanage multiplication. You can't oversee every hand that touches what God is spreading. You have to trust that the same God who delivered it through you is capable of multiplying it beyond you.

Just like Hannah had to release Samuel, you need to release this baby.

MOSES DELIVERED. JOSHUA MULTIPLIED.

Look at Moses. He led Israel out of Egypt. That was his assignment. But Moses didn't enter the Promised Land. Joshua carried the people into multiplication.

Moses had to be secure enough to obey his portion and trust that God would finish the work through someone else.

Multiplication often happens through others God assigns to carry the promise forward. You don't have to see every piece to know that God's plan is unfolding.

YOU AREN'T THE SOURCE. YOU'RE THE VESSEL.

The moment you think the promise depends on you, you'll start trying to control outcomes you were never responsible for.

God chose you to carry it. God chose you to lead it. But God is still the source. He controls the multiplication.

You are responsible for obedience. He is responsible for impact.

MULTIPLICATION WILL LOOK DIFFERENT THAN YOU EXPECT

This is where your faith gets tested again.

Multiplication won't always look like your version of growth. It may come through people you didn't expect. It may reach places you never imagined. It may open doors you didn't pray for.

And that's exactly how God planned it.

If it stayed small enough for you to control, it wouldn't be multiplication. It would be maintenance.

MULTIPLICATION ISN'T ABOUT YOUR NAME

Here's the real test of your heart.

Can you handle the fact that your obedience may bless people who never know your name? Can you celebrate that your yes is feeding people who may never send you a thank you?

If you need credit to stay obedient, you're not ready for multiplication.

God called you to build something that outlives you, not something that spotlights you.

YOU WON'T SEE THE FULL HARVEST IN THIS LIFE

Some of what you birthed won't reach full bloom until after you're gone.

That's not discouraging. That's legacy.

God builds through generations. The seeds you planted through prayer, sacrifice, and obedience will continue producing long after you've stepped into eternity.

That's multiplication.

YOU DELIVERED THE SEED. GOD DELIVERS THE HARVEST.

Paul said it best in 1 Corinthians 3:6:

"I planted, Apollos watered, but God was causing the growth."

You planted. You watered. Now God is multiplying. Your assignment was never small. You just didn't see how far the roots would go.

PRAYER

Lord, I release control of what You've birthed through me. Multiply the promise according to Your plan. Help me stay surrendered as You expand it beyond what I can see.Keep my heart pure when the growth exceeds my control. I trust You to multiply the seed You planted. In Jesus' name, Amen.

REFLECTION QUESTIONS

1. Where have you struggled to release control as God multiplies your assignment?

2. How can you stay surrendered when multiplication takes forms you didn't expect?

3. Are you willing to trust God for results even when you don't

receive personal credit?

Chapter 23

THE MIDWIFE MANTLE: HELPING OTHERS BIRTH THEIR ASSIGNMENT

You made it through your labor. You delivered what God put inside you. You learned how to carry, push, raise, and release. And now you thought you could sit down and relax.

Not quite.

Because now you've entered a new season. God isn't just calling you to carry your own promise. He's calling you to help someone else deliver theirs.

You've moved from laborer to midwife.

YOU DIDN'T GO THROUGH ALL THAT JUST FOR YOU

The warfare you fought, the lessons you learned, the mistakes you made, and the wisdom you gained were never supposed to stay trapped inside your journal.

God doesn't waste pain. He doesn't waste pressure. He doesn't waste your process. Everything you went through is now a tool to help somebody else get through their own delivery.

You survived so you could serve.

MIDWIVES KNOW WHAT LABOR FEELS LIKE

The reason you're qualified to help others is because you've been where they are.

You know the frustration of waiting. You know the fear of stepping out. You know the pressure of carrying something bigger than you. You know the exhaustion that hits when nothing seems to be moving.

That experience gives you authority. You don't have to guess what they're feeling. You've lived it.

MIDWIVES DON'T PUSH FOR THE WOMAN

Let's get one thing straight.

Being a midwife does not mean doing the pushing for somebody else. You can't deliver their promise for them.

Your job is to coach, encourage, and guide. You create a safe space for them to push. You don't do the pushing yourself. If you try to carry what they're called to birth, you'll both end up exhausted.

Support doesn't mean substitution.

MIDWIVES DON'T COMPETE WITH THE WOMAN IN LABOR

You're not there to shine. You're not there to steal the moment. You're not there to showcase your own wisdom while they're trying to survive contractions.

This is not your delivery. It's theirs. Your job is to serve without making it about you.

Real midwives don't need credit. They know their assignment is vital even if nobody sees it.

MIDWIVES STAY CALM WHEN THE PRESSURE HITS

Labor gets messy. There will be moments when the woman you're helping wants to quit. She'll say things she doesn't mean. She'll cry. She'll doubt. She'll panic.

Your job is not to match her panic. Your job is to stay steady.

You remind her of what's on the other side. You remind her of what God said. You remind her that quitting is not an option. You hold space for her weakness while pointing her back to God's strength.

MIDWIVES PROTECT THE ROOM

You've already learned that not everyone belongs in the birthing room. Now, as a midwife, you help guard the atmosphere for others.

You shut down voices that bring fear. You cover the assignment in prayer. You discern who has access and who doesn't. You keep distractions out so delivery can happen.

Sometimes your greatest service is protecting the room while God works.

MIDWIVES KNOW WHEN TO STEP BACK

When the promise finally comes forth, you celebrate, but you don't make it about yourself.

You don't attach yourself to their assignment. You don't expect access to what they delivered just because you helped them push.

A good midwife celebrates the birth without claiming ownership of the baby.

GOD TRUSTS MIDWIVES WITH HOLY WORK

Helping someone deliver their assignment is sacred. You are partnering with Heaven to see purpose fulfilled in someone else's life. That kind of work requires maturity, humility, and discernment.

You've graduated from carrying your own assignment to now becoming a safe place for others to carry theirs. That's legacy.

PRAYER

Lord, teach me how to serve as a midwife for others.Give me wisdom to coach without controlling. Keep my heart humble as I help others birth what You've planted in them. Use my testimony as a tool to encourage and equip. Protect my motives and keep me focused on Your glory, not my own. In Jesus' name, Amen.

REFLECTION QUESTIONS

1. Who has God assigned you to help in their birthing process?

2. Where have you struggled to stay in your lane as a midwife rather than trying to control the process?

3. How can you create a safe, faith-filled environment for others to deliver their assignments?

Chapter 24
THE LEGACY: YOUR LABOR WAS FOR GENERATIONS

You thought this was about one promise. One assignment. One moment.

It wasn't.

God never called you to birth something that stops with you. He called you to leave something that outlives you.

That is legacy.

LEGACY ISN'T BUILT ON MOMENTS. IT'S BUILT ON OBEDIENCE.

You didn't create legacy when you posted your launch announcement. You created legacy when you obeyed in silence.

Legacy was built when you stayed consistent while nobody was watching. Legacy was built when you kept praying when you wanted to quit. Legacy was built when you disciplined yourself to carry what God gave you even when it cost you everything.

The fruit you see today is the result of private yeses nobody clapped for.

YOUR OBEDIENCE BECAME SOMEBODY ELSE'S FOUNDATION

The yes you fought for is now the floor somebody else will stand on.

There are women coming behind you who will walk further because you broke ground they couldn't see. There are children, spiritual and natural, who will carry assignments because you were faithful enough to carry yours. There are people who will be delivered because you wouldn't abandon your process when it got hard.

They may never know all the battles you fought. But they will walk in the freedom your obedience produced.

LEGACY REQUIRES FORESIGHT, NOT JUST PASSION

It's easy to stay passionate in the moment. Passion is emotional. Passion fades.

Legacy requires discipline. It asks you to build with tomorrow in mind, not just today's emotions.

You're not managing a project. You're stewarding something God intends to keep producing long after you're gone.

LEGACY FORCES YOU TO THINK DIFFERENTLY ABOUT SUCCESS

You start asking different questions.

You stop asking, "How big can I build it? "You start asking, "How strong can I leave it?"

You stop asking, "Who's noticing me?" You start asking, "Who's equipped to carry this after me?"

Legacy shifts your focus from visibility to sustainability.

You're not trying to be famous. You're trying to be faithful.

GOD THINKS IN GENERATIONS

From the very beginning, God has always worked generationally.

He identified Himself as the God of Abraham, Isaac, and Jacob. Not the God of one person. The God of lineage. The God of legacy.

Your assignment is a thread in a much larger story God is writing through your family, your ministry, your spiritual children, and your obedience.

What you build now affects people you may never meet.

YOU MAY NOT SEE THE FULL HARVEST, AND THAT'S OKAY

Let's settle this now.

Some of the fruit God produces through your obedience won't show up while you're alive. You won't see every life your labor touches. You won't know every breakthrough your yes creates.

But you can trust that Heaven is keeping perfect records. Nothing you've carried, birthed, raised, or released will be wasted.

Psalm 145:4 says:

"One generation will praise Your works to another and declare Your mighty acts."

That's legacy.

LEGACY ISN'T JUST WHAT YOU BUILD. IT'S WHO YOU BECAME.

At the end of all this, your legacy won't just be about your ministry, your business, your book, or your platform.

It will be about the woman you became through the process.

The woman who surrendered when it was hard.The woman who obeyed when it was scary. The woman who trusted God when it didn't make sense. The woman who delivered purpose even when labor nearly broke her.

That woman is your legacy too.

PRAYER

Lord, help me build beyond myself.Give me wisdom to lead with future generations in mind. Let my obedience create open doors for those who come after me. Keep my heart anchored in faithfulness, not fame. May everything I birth continue producing long after I'm gone. In Jesus' name, Amen.

REFLECTION QUESTIONS

1. How has your thinking shifted from personal success to lasting legacy?

2. Who in your life is being impacted by your obedience right now?

3. What systems or foundations can you build to protect the assignment for future generations?

Chapter 25
THE BENEDICTION: YOU WERE MADE TO CARRY THIS

Look at you.

You carried it. You survived the waiting room. You endured the s tretching.You travailed. You pushed.You delivered.You raised it. You released it. You multiplied it. You protected the room. You stayed faithful when you could have folded.

And now you stand here, on the other side of what you once feared would break you.

YOU DIDN'T IMAGINE THIS. YOU WERE BUILT FOR THIS.

There were days you questioned if you heard God right. There were moments you wondered if you made it all up. There were nights you sat in silence thinking, "Maybe I'm not strong enough for this."

And now you can see it for what it always was.

This was never about your strength. This was always about God's grace pulling you through what He trusted you to carry.

THE FACT THAT YOU SURVIVED IS PROOF THAT YOU WERE CHOSEN

If this was too heavy for you, you wouldn't still be standing. If you weren't equipped, you would've dropped it long ago. If you weren't called, you would have walked away the first time it cost you more than you expected.

But you stayed. You carried.You delivered.

That alone is evidence that God knew what He was doing when He picked you.

YOU DON'T HAVE TO BE PERFECT TO BE CHOSEN

Let's clear this up once and for all.

You stumbled. You cried. You doubted. You delayed sometimes. You second-guessed. You got in your own head. You fought fear more than you want to admit.

But none of that disqualified you.

God doesn't pick people based on flawless execution. He picks people based on surrendered hearts. That's what He saw in you.

THIS WAS NEVER JUST ABOUT THE PROMISE. IT WAS ABOUT YOUR PARTNERSHIP.

Yes, you delivered the assignment. But something bigger happened in the process. You became someone God can trust with the next thing.

You learned how to partner with Him in the middle of pressure.You learned how to carry what didn't make sense.You learned how to trust Him with what was too heavy for you.

That partnership will carry you through every new season He calls you into from this moment forward.

YOU CAN REST IN THE FACT THAT GOD KNEW EXACTLY WHO HE WAS PICKING

From the first moment He placed this seed inside of you, He factored in everything.

Your personality.Your weaknesses. Your mistakes.Your background.Y our fears.Your flaws. Your delays. Your stubborn moments. Your fragile seasons.

And He still said, "You."

That's why you're standing here now. That's why the promise didn't die in the waiting. That's why the assignment made it to full-term. Because He never questioned if you could carry it. Only you did.

YOU WERE MADE TO CARRY THIS

Not because you were the smartest. Not because you were the most talented. Not because you had the biggest platform.

You were made to carry this because you were willing to say yes.

You didn't have to know how. You just had to trust Who. And you did.

YOUR FINAL PRAYER

Lord, thank You for trusting me to carry what You planted in me. Thank You for the strength to endure, the grace to obey, and the power to deliver. I surrender my assignment fully to You. I will continue to steward what You've placed in my hands with humility, wisdom, and courage. And I will trust You for whatever You assign me to carry next. In Jesus' name, Amen.

FINAL REFLECTION

Take a moment to breathe. You carried what many would have abandoned.

This isn't the end. This is only the end of this labor. The God who brought you through this is faithful to lead you into the next.

You were made for this.

Chapter 26
About the Author

Diane Ferreira is a Bible teacher, coach, speaker, and published author who serves as a spiritual midwife for women carrying God-sized assignments. Known for her bold, no-nonsense voice and her ability to mix deep biblical teaching with real-life humor, Diane helps women step into the hard, holy work of delivering what God has placed inside them.

She is passionate about equipping women to recognize the weight of their calling without being crushed by it. Her teaching combines truth, clarity, and the kind of sass that feels like having coffee with a friend who refuses to let you quit.

Diane is the author of Confessions of a Word Girl, The Messy Middle Manual, The New Jerusalem, and Your Bible Uncomplicated. Each project reflects her heart to make biblical truth accessible, practical, and applicable for real life.

She is the co-founder of She Opens Her Bible™, Affirm Faith Co.™, and the She's So Scripture™ Substack community, where she continues to pour into women through writing, teaching, and coaching.

Diane lives with her husband and their extremely entitled bulldog, Gronk, who remains convinced that he runs the house while generously allowing the humans to stay.

Also by Diane Ferreira

Also by Diane Ferreira

The Proverbs 31-ish Woman

A hilarious, grace-drenched guide for every perfectly imperfect woman of faith who's trying to walk holy without losing her whole mind.

Holy, Hormonal & Holding On

Because being spiritually grounded and emotionally unpredictable can *totally* coexist. This devotional keeps it real, raw, and redeemed.

The Messy Middle Manual

A soulful survival guide for women navigating the in-between—when you're not where you were, but not yet where you're going.

The New Jerusalem

A poetic and prophetic portrait of heaven's promise and the restoration we're all aching for.

Confessions of a Word Girl

For every woman with a Bible, a bold voice, and the guts to speak her truth with scripture as her mic.

Stay Connected:

Visit ValeAndVinePress.com
Subscribe to *She's So Scripture* on Substack

www.ingramcontent.com/pod-product-compliance
Lightning Source LLC
Chambersburg PA
CBHW070323130626
46556CB00007B/2713